The Sierra Club Kid's Guide to
Planet Care & Repair

The Sierra Club Kid's Guide to
Planet Care & Repair

Vicki McVey

Illustrated by Martha Weston

SIERRA CLUB BOOKS FOR CHILDREN

San Francisco

First Edition

All maps by Vicki McVey

Library of Congress Cataloging-in-Publication Data
McVey, Vicki.
       The Sierra Club kid's guide to planet care and repair / Vicki McVey; illustrated by Martha Weston.
              p.   cm.
       Includes index.
       Summary: Explains how human activities are destroying the balance of nature and suggests ways to prevent further damage.
       ISBN 0-87156-567-6
       1. Environmental protection — Citizen participation — Juvenile literature.   2. Ecology — Juvenile literature.   3. Human ecology — Juvenile literature.   [1. Environmental protection.   2. Man — Influence on nature.]   I. Weston, Martha, ill.   II. Title.
TD171.7.M385   1992
363.7'0525 — dc20   91-38307

Printed in the United States of America on acid-free paper containing 50 percent recovered waste.

10   9   8   7   6   5   4   3   2   1

To Mom and Sally,
because they love Mother Earth

To Susan,
because she thought of it

Contents

The Sierra Club Kid's Guide to
Planet Care & Repair

1

Our Voyage on the Earth-ship

What is Earth? To an astronomer, it's the third planet from the sun. To a biologist, it's the only planet that's known to support life. To a historian, it's the place where human history has unfolded. To all of us, it's home.

But not too many years ago, a man named Buckminster Fuller (who, besides being an architect and an engineer, was a person who wrote and talked about a lot of different things) came up with a new way of thinking about Earth. Our planet, according to Fuller, is a huge, living spaceship, and we are all astronauts, traveling on it through space.

If you could think up the most amazing space vehicle of all time, it still couldn't compare to the one we're traveling on. Our Earth-ship is 5 billion years old, measures almost 25,000 miles around the middle, and travels at 18½ miles per second. It has billions and billions of parts, both living and nonliving, all working together in a perfectly coordinated system.

Until recently, we humans thought we were just along for the ride — or worse, that we were actually in charge of the voyage. No one knew that the human race was really a part of the Earth-ship. We didn't realize that we — and all the other parts of our ship — were directly linked to its life support system, and that we couldn't do anything without in some way affecting the ship as a whole.

Here is an exercise for your imagination: What if you were traveling through space on a star-ship and you discovered that, because you and the other passengers didn't really understand the ship's system, you were doing things that seriously damaged it? Some living parts of the system were dying, and many other parts were malfunctioning because of either neglect or misuse.

What would you do? Would you pretend that you didn't know, not tell anyone else, and keep on doing things the same old way? Or would you tell your fellow travelers what you had discovered and then try to figure out what to do about it?

Well, we Earthlings have actually made a similar discovery about our own ship. And now, in order to help repair past mistakes and keep from making new ones, each one of us needs to learn about Earth's system and how our own behavior may affect it.

One of the most important things to know about any system, whether it is as small as an atom or as big as the universe, is that all of its parts are connected. John Muir, a man who spent most of his life studying nature and trying to get people to pay attention to its systems, once said, "When we try to pick out anything by itself, we find it hitched to everything else in the universe." As you go through this book and observe how things work, you will discover for yourself some of the connections that John Muir was talking about.

Earth's system is so finely balanced and complicated that, when it is changed (as we humans are likely to change it), it's hard to know in advance what the results of that change will be. But we are learning that a change we make in one part of the system may echo through the rest of it, and may finally bounce back and hit us over the head. Here is a true story about how that works.

On the Hawaiian Islands there is a large toad called a cane toad. It got that name because it lives in sugarcane fields and eats a type of grub worm that would otherwise chew up and eventually kill the sugarcane crops. So the cane toad, in Hawaii, is a very helpful sort of amphibian.

Well, some sugarcane farmers in Australia decided to take care of their own grub worm problem once and for all. They sent to Hawaii for a shipment of cane toads, turned them loose in a pond in the middle of some cane fields, and said good-bye to their grub worms.

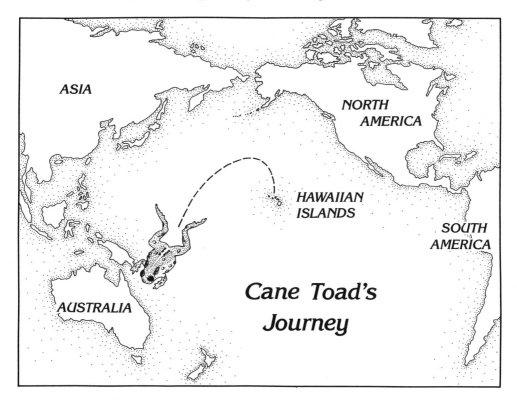

But as soon as the toads arrived in Australia, they stopped being Hawaiian cane toads and became Australian cane toads. That's not so surprising. What did surprise the Australian farmers was that the cane toads, when they changed citizenship, lost their taste for grub worms and began eating everything else in sight.

So the Australian farmers not only had to contend with grub worms, they also had to find something that would eat the huge cane toads. Unfortunately, when they tried to feed the toads to various other hungry animals, they discovered that cane toads have a handy self-defense strategy. They manufacture poison inside their bodies and shoot it at anything that threatens them.

Now, since there are no other creatures to eat them, the cane toads have multiplied and become a bigger problem than the grub worms were to begin with. Of course the story is much more complicated than that, but the moral is still clear. The Australian farmers made a mistake that is easy to see with hindsight, but almost impossible to see in advance. They changed the system without understanding how all of its parts worked.

A CANE TOAD IS ABOUT THIS SIZE.

We all do that every day: When we ride in our cars, we add to the pollution of the atmosphere, which is one of the most important parts of Earth's system. When we flush our toilets unnecessarily, we waste water that is urgently needed for other uses (and is another basic part of Earth's system). It's not that we have to get rid of things like cars and toilets; we just need to redesign them or use them differently so they won't damage our system.

Finding a way to do that will be difficult, but not impossible. Look at it this way: Our system took 5 billion years to develop, and in all that time it has been recycling its own raw materials over and over again. The water you are using today may have been drunk by Cleopatra or Alexander the Great! Your job is to make sure that when you are through with it, it isn't so contaminated that people in the future can't use it in their turn.

There is no problem with using the resources that our system provides. Everything alive consumes its environment. Every time we eat, drink, breathe, or just walk in the sunlight, we take part of the environment into our own individual systems. Consumption is a problem only if we take more than our share and waste some of it, or if our use of a resource destroys it for future consumption or creates damaging by-products (like pollution or unexpected reactions in the system).

It's too bad that most of the human travelers on the Earth-ship are still ignoring the damage they're doing to its systems. But the good news is that many other people *are* taking responsibility for the care of our planet. Some of these people run the governments of the world, making decisions that affect millions of lives; some work quietly in their own fields or backyards. Many are children.

Planet care and repair seems like a huge job for you, me, or anyone. But fortunately for us, and for Planet Earth, we already have the tools we need: bodies that can go almost anywhere and collect information about the world outside; brains that use that information for recognizing and solving problems; and "hearts" that know how to love and take care of things.

This book is a guide that will show you how to use the tools you already have to help care for and maintain our Earth-ship. It is also a book of stories about people, mostly children, who are doing just that. (Although all the stories are based on real facts, the children and some of the events in them are made up.) You might be surprised at how much one single person can accomplish, and if you add the energy of several individual people together, amazing things can happen.

At the end of most chapters there will be projects, activities, games, or special tips to teach you about the Earth-ship, or about basic planet care.

Journal

A small notebook makes a good journal for recording your experiences as you go through this book. There will be some specific experiments to make notes on, and you might want to write about your feelings and adventures as you learn more about our amazing Earth-ship.

2

Energy Makes It Run

Have you ever stopped to think about what keeps you going — about what your own power source is? Every system has to have one, or it would just run down. If you trace the fuel supply back far enough, the system called your body has the same power source as the system called Earth.

Even though you might get energy directly from your last peanut butter and jelly sandwich, the peanuts in the peanut butter, the fruit and sugar in the jelly, and the wheat in the bread all got *their* energy from the sun. In fact, all systems on our planet, from the entire Earth-ship itself down to the tiny microbe in your left ear, are powered by the sun.

Solar energy leaves the sun and travels through space in waves of heat, light, and other useful forms of radiation. All that energy is cycled through our planet's various systems (including your own body), and then it's sent back into space. It's an ongoing process: The sun continues beaming radiation, and the Earth-ship keeps using it for power and then returning it to space.

Here's a good question: If the sun beams energy to our planet automatically, and it's going to keep beaming it for billions of years, how is it possible to waste it? How can you waste something that not only is free, but comes in unlimited supply?

The answer is that the Earth-ship has been converting the sun's energy into different "storage units" for billions of years, and it's the storage units that we're wasting. A tree, for instance, in addition to being an amazing and wonderful life-form, is a solar storage unit. If you cut down a tree, you can recover the energy that's in it and use it to warm yourself, cook your food, and feed your goats, as well as to build your house.

Of course, you can grow another tree to replace the one you cut down (even though very few people actually do that) and keep a steady supply of solar storage units for future use. Since trees *can* be replaced as they are used, they make up what is called a *renewable* energy source. But there are other solar storage units — other forms of energy — that are *nonrenewable*. Once you use them, they're gone for good. Among the various nonrenewable forms of energy are those called *fossil fuels* ("fossil" because they are made of plants that died and decomposed millions of years ago, and "fuels" because they are used as a power source).

Fossil fuels, including coal, oil, and gas, are among our planet's major sources of energy, but we are finding out that burning them causes serious problems. One of those problems is pollution.

When people first began burning coal about two hundred years ago, during the Industrial Revolution, they had no idea that this could cause a buildup of carbon dioxide in the atmosphere, which, in turn, could lead to higher temperatures and changing climates all over the world (you'll find out how that works in Chapter 9). Now we know that burning fossil fuels puts dangerous stress on the Earth-ship's life support system, but we have become dependent on them for energy. It's going to be difficult to develop other sources of fuel.

As reserves of fossil fuels have been used up, and as they have gotten more expensive to extract and transport, people have looked for other ways to generate energy. One of these "energy alternatives" is the production of electricity using a nuclear reaction.

You've probably heard of nuclear energy, and chances are that what you've heard about it lately isn't good. In the 1950s, many people thought that the answers to all our energy problems were going to be found in the development of nuclear power. But we have since discovered that there are serious problems linked to the production of nuclear energy. One of them is the possible release of radioactive materials during a nuclear accident, such as the one that occurred in 1986 at the Chernobyl power plant in Russia.

We have also learned that, while the process of splitting atoms produces a huge amount of energy fairly cheaply, it generates something called "radioactive waste," and there is no safe place to put this deadly by-product of nuclear fission. The only way to safely get rid of radioactivity is to wait for it to decay naturally. The problem is that it takes anywhere from hundreds of thousands to millions of years for this natural process to happen!

Of course, it's possible to seal radioactive waste material in a container and then dump it in the sea or bury it underground, but what kind of container will last for a million or more years? It's one of those problems that we don't yet have the technology to solve.

Although nuclear energy hasn't turned out to be the easy answer it was originally thought to be, there are other alternative forms of energy that neither depend on fossil fuels nor produce dangerous by-products. One of these is good old solar energy.

Electricity that comes from the burning of fossil fuels costs from five to seven cents per kilowatt-hour and accounts for 30 percent of the carbon dioxide that we pump into the atmosphere here in the United States. (A kilowatt-hour is a way of measuring electricity. A refrigerator, for instance, uses about seven kilowatt-hours of electricity per day.) For just a little bit more money (eight cents per kilowatt-hour), it's possible to generate electricity by using the sun — and this form of energy doesn't pollute at all.

Right now there isn't a very strong push to explore solar power, partly because the technology for storing large quantities of solar energy cheaply and easily hasn't been developed yet. But in not too many years, people your age will be making the decisions. You'll be able to elect government officials who support solar energy research. Maybe you'll even become a solar engineer, or an architect who designs solar homes.

Another nonpolluting alternative energy source is the wind. If you think of sailboats and windmills, you'll realize that there is nothing new about using wind as a source of energy. California is currently the world's largest producer of wind power, generating almost 3 billion kilowatt-hours of electricity using windmills each year. That sounds like a tremendous amount, but it's actually less than 2 percent of the electricity that Californians use.

Have you ever seen a problem turned into a solution? Using garbage to produce energy is just such a case. Landfills (or "dumps") naturally produce a certain amount of methane gas as the garbage in them decomposes. In some places, that gas has been trapped, run through pipes, and then used as fuel. Since methane gas can actually be a pollutant if it is released into the atmosphere, this solution takes care of three problems: It gets rid of garbage, it generates energy, and it cuts down on the amount of methane going up into the air.

SOLAR POWER PANELS FOR HOME ELECTRICITY

Another clean way of making electricity is with water power. Hydroelectric power, generated by waterfalls and rapidly moving rivers, provides about one-third of the world's electricity. But this form of energy is not without problems of its own. For one, water that is to be used to make electricity must often be dammed first. Hydroelectric dams have buried hundreds of thousands of acres of land under tons of water. In some parts of the world, entire villages have been submerged and their inhabitants left to start all over again in new places. This has caused serious problems in areas such as the Amazon basin in South America.

Although many of these alternative energy options have tremendous promise for the future, right now the greatest hope for reducing our dependence on fossil fuels lies in energy efficiency. This means finding ways to reduce the amount of energy it takes to get any particular job done. There are two main areas where this can happen: in our homes and in our transportation systems.

One of the best ways that you, personally, can help take care of our planet is to be very careful about how you use energy at home. We need to heat and cool our houses, for instance, but we don't need to waste energy in the process.

Here is an interesting experiment to do on a cold and windy day: Light a candle inside your house and take a walk with it. Go anyplace inside where you can feel a draft — from around windows, under doors, and through electrical wall plates on outside walls, for instance. You can probably think of lots of places to check. If the candle flame wavers after you have stopped moving, then your family is using energy to try to heat the air outside your house — and that is a losing proposition!

Once you discover where the air leaks are, you can find lots of ways to fix them. You can help someone put up a layer of clear plastic inside windows, plug up unused electrical outlets, or close the damper when the fireplace isn't being used. Every winter, as much energy leaks out of windows in the United States as flows through the Alaskan pipeline in one year. If you and your family are careful, it won't be your hot air that's escaping.

How often has someone asked you to turn off the lights when you leave a room (or maybe you're the one to ask other people in your family)? It's a good habit to get into. Another way to save electricity is to use compact fluorescent light bulbs (available from several mail-order companies) instead of the standard incandescent bulbs we're all used to. Compact fluorescents use about one-quarter of the energy of regular bulbs, and they burn ten or more times longer. Though they're more expensive to begin with, you'll still come out ahead.

There's no question that burning fossil fuels to run transportation is a primary stress on the Earth-ship's life support system. In the United States there are almost enough cars for every single person — child and adult — to have one of his or her own. In China, on the other hand, there is only one car for every 1,374 people. China and India together make up a little over one-third of the world's population, but they have only one-half of 1 percent of its cars.

So how do people in those countries get around? Well, it has two wheels and two handles, and it requires a certain amount of concentration and balance to ride. You guessed it: a bike. In China, there are 540 bicycles for every car — and that adds up to about one bike for every four people. Since bikes take up much less space than cars, don't pollute the atmosphere, and require no external energy source (besides their owners' legs), they are a great alternative to cars.

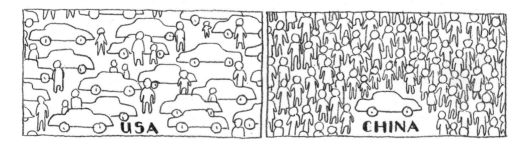

Something that you can do for our planet is consider transportation alternatives. When you need to go somewhere, instead of asking an adult to take you in the car, ride your bike, walk, or take the bus. Here's a story about a kid who created his own business around a transportation alternative:

Jerome, who lived in Cleveland, Ohio, was learning some things in his social studies class that were beginning to make him mad. It seemed to him that many of the thoughtless systems that had been created by people before he was even born were going to ruin the world.

One day his mother was getting ready to take the car on a short errand, and Jerome blew up. "Mom, every time you turn on the car you're spewing junk into the air. I mean dangerous, toxic junk! Man, this really stinks!"

"Well, Jerome," his mother said quietly, "why don't you do something about it?"

Oh, right, he thought. I don't even *drive*! I'm a bicycle freak.

Actually, Jerome was a bicycle racer — and a good one, too. He had won several important local races, and he had earned the money himself to buy his current racing bike (he also had a junker that he used for basic transportation). Now, as usual when he was agitated, he got on his bike and peeled away to ride as fast as he could.

Jerome always did his best thinking on a bike. In fact, he sometimes wondered if his anatomy had gotten mixed up and his brains were in his feet. As the world rushed by his ears, he thought about what his mother had said. It had seemed really silly at first, but what if he *could* do something? He definitely had strong feelings and, as usual, more energy than he knew what to do with. After a while he hatched an idea:

JEROME'S TAXI BIKE

Geneneral errand, grocery, and small-child transport service.

This ain't no jive—
you don't need to drive.

Just pay my fare
and save the air.

"Jerome's Taxi Bike," a general errand and small-child transportation service.

He already had a kiddie seat for his little brother on the back of his junker bike, and he added a basket to the handlebars. Then he put a small ad in the local paper and asked his parents to tell their friends. He also mentioned his new business to the parents of his own friends. He got a real break when his ad caught the eye of a local reporter. She called and told him she had been attracted by his rhyming jingle, and she ended up writing a story for the Sunday magazine about Jerome's business and the reason behind it.

He got so many calls that he had to hire one of his friends to help him during the busy times of the day. And even though it hadn't been his intention, he ended up earning money. Everyone thought his anti-pollution business was great, and he was surprised at the number of people who hired him because they just wanted to support the idea behind it.

There are lots of things that you, yourself, can do to help support the Earth-ship. If you would like to experiment with alternative energy, for instance, here is a project that will show you how.

Solar Hot Dogs

It might seem a little extreme to build a solar cooker just to cook a hot dog, but this project will give you an idea of how easy it is to harvest the sun's energy. You'll need a cardboard box, about 1 or 1½ feet square and about 6 inches deep; some aluminum foil; some black paper or paint; and one or more coat hangers.

To make the solar cooker, first cover the outside of the box with black paper (or paint it black), and then line the inside with aluminum foil. Now straighten out the coat hanger and poke it through opposite sides of the box, about an inch from the top, so it runs across the inside of the box (see the picture below).

Your solar cooker will work best in the middle of a sunny day. To use it, pull the coat hanger out of the box, put a couple of hot dogs on it, and then stick the hanger back in with the hot dogs over the inside of the box. Put the box in a sunny place and wait until the hot dogs are sizzling hot (5–10 minutes).

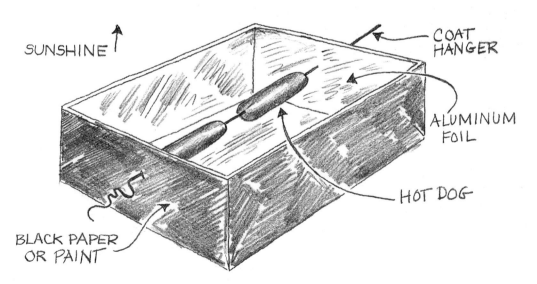

SUNSHINE

COAT HANGER

ALUMINUM FOIL

HOT DOG

BLACK PAPER OR PAINT

3

Water, Water Everywhere...

Maybe our planet should have been called "Water" instead of "Earth." After all, nearly three-quarters of it is covered with the huge bodies of water-in-motion that we call oceans. These oceans help regulate the global climate, they provide us with many types of food and mineral nutrients, and they are the original source of our freshwater supplies. The oceans are also full of rich and beautiful environments teeming with life.

Our planet's oceans are a vital part of the system called Earth, and they also have smaller systems within them. There's a useful word that describes all the parts of any environmental system, both living and nonliving, that interact together. That word is *ecosystem*. An ecosystem can be as simple as a lichen-covered rock in the middle of the frozen Arctic, or as complicated as a coral reef off the coast of Australia. In either case, all of its parts developed together over many thousands of years, and they still interact and depend on one another.

Ocean (or marine) ecosystems are among the most fascinating on Earth. And some marine ecosystems are among the most fragile. Since everything in the system is tied together, if we change one part, the rest of it will also be changed.

16

One way we are changing marine ecosystems is by overfishing them. What that usually means is that we remove so many fish of one particular species that the species has a hard time recovering. Here is an example of how that works:

Although most of us think of sharks as "dangerous" rather than as "endangered," their numbers are being seriously depleted in parts of Earth's oceans. Shark meat has become such a popular item in stores and restaurants in the United States that sharks are being overfished in some U.S. coastal waters. And in the North Pacific, blue sharks (along with other animals such as dolphins and seabirds) are accidently caught in the huge drift nets of Japanese, Korean, and Taiwanese fishing boats. These vessels are intended to catch squid, but most of the creatures caught in their nets are unwanted *by-catch*. These animals are then thrown back, usually dead, into the ocean.

Drift net fishing is so devastating to marine ecosystems that many environmental groups and government organizations are working to have it outlawed. In the meantime, thousands of blue sharks are caught in drift nets, and because their tails and dorsal fins are used to make shark fin soup, those parts are cut off and the sharks are dumped back into the ocean.

No one knows what would happen to the marine ecosystems if all the sharks were destroyed, but, unlovable as they are, sharks play a crucial part in keeping these systems in balance. In fact, it is probably safe to assume that most of the creatures that share the planet with us are important to the smooth running of the Earth-ship.

Although overfishing is certainly a great threat to marine ecosystems, it is not the only human activity that creates problems. If you live on or near a coast, or watch the news from time to time, you can probably think of several other things we are doing to endanger the world's oceans.

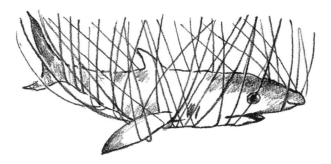

Can you imagine how you would feel if you were swimming in a pool and a dump truck backed up to the edge of the water and tipped a huge load of smelly garbage into it? Believe it or not, people do that. Not into swimming pools, but into the world's oceans, which is actually much worse. Our garbage often contains poisonous chemicals that threaten the lives of the creatures that live in the water, and sometimes even our own.

Here are some hair-raising statistics: The city of New York dumps 2,600 tons of carbon, 870 tons of oil and grease, 520 tons of nitrogen, 230 tons of iron, 13.8 tons of copper, and 12.7 tons of lead into the ocean *every day* — not to mention tons and tons of organic garbage, including human waste. Can you imagine *anything* (except possibly the New York Bight Slime Creature) surviving in that water?

Ocean currents carry pollutants thousands of miles from where they are dumped, and all kinds of strange and terrible things find their way into the stomachs of marine animals, even animals that live in the middle of the world's largest oceans.

There are two important things we can do to improve this awful situation: First, we can produce less garbage (there will be more about that in Chapter 11); and second, we can create stricter regulations. Something that is beginning to make a difference in the regulation of ocean dumping is space technology. Images taken from space-roving satellites are now tracing the flow of dangerous pollutants. With this new technology, it is easier both to monitor ocean dumping and to get the support of lawmakers to create stricter regulations.

On the next page is a game that will let you be an environmental activist and go on your own journey over the oceans to collect information. After that is a suggestion for a way to hook up with an organization that is cleaning up the ocean shores.

Save the Sea Game

To play this game, you need two people and the following materials: two pieces of paper (with books or magazines under them to write on), two pencils, a ruler, and four markers (red, black, blue, and orange). Since this is a grid game, you'll each have to draw a grid like the one shown below. Here's how the game works:

You each belong to an environmental organization that sends fact-finding teams out to document activities suspected of being destructive to the marine ecosystems. One of you represents Friends of the Sea, and the other represents Ocean-to-Ocean.

On your own grid, you are each going to position the following activities for the other to find: burial of radioactive waste, drift net fishing, whaling, and pollution entering the sea. Each of these activities will be represented by a colored circle that you will mark at a grid intersection.

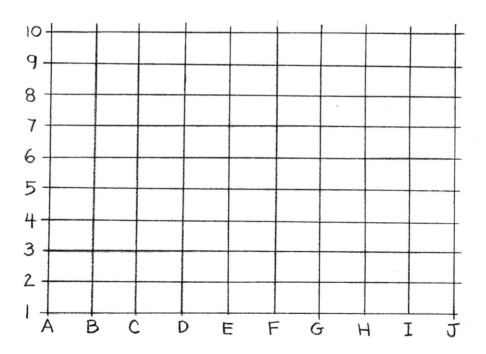

You will mark three sites for each activity (making sure the other person doesn't see where they are): three red circles for pollution entering the sea, three black circles for drift net fishing, three blue circles for whaling, and three orange circles for radioactive waste burial. After you have marked the circles, put a key near the bottom of your grid to remind you of what the different colors mean.

Next, letter and number your grids as shown on page 19, so that each intersection, where the lines cross, has a specific "address." For instance, "4D" is the place where the line 4 and the line D cross each other.

To play the game, each of you, in turn, tries to find the circled locations on the other's grid. During each turn, you will guess one intersection — 7F, for instance. Your friend will check on her or his grid to see if there is a circle there. If there is, you must then guess what kind of activity you have located. (If you don't get it right on the first try, you must wait for your next turn to try to identify the activity.) As soon as you successfully guess a location, your friend will cross out that circle on his or her grid, and you will mark it on your own grid so that you won't guess it again. The first person to locate all the circles on the other person's grid wins the game.

Beach Cleanup

If you happen to live near the ocean, you might want to contact the Center for Marine Conservation, 1725 Desales Street NW, Washington, DC 20036. This organization sponsors a nationwide three-hour beach cleanup every year on the third Saturday of September. One year people all around the United States picked up *2 million pounds* of trash in just three hours! (That's especially impressive since most of it was plastic, which doesn't weigh very much.) If the people in your community aren't already part of this effort, maybe you could help get them involved.

4

...But Not a Drop to Drink?

Imagine a desert — a parched landscape, shimmering like flames. You are lost, looking for any kind of shade to hide in. You finally crawl into a wide crack at the base of a cliff. The last of your water barely wet your throat several hours ago, and now your mouth is like a dry tunnel sucking heat into your body.

You lie down and close your eyes, too exhausted to sleep. The desert is so quiet you can hear your heart beat, and you think of the liquid it is pumping. *Thump...thump...thump*, like a steady pulse.

But gradually you become aware of another sound: *drip...drip... drip*. Your eyes jump open and you move so fast your head cracks against the rock overhang. You force your body further inside the hollow, and the dripping sound is louder. Something small and cold hits your ear and slides inside it. You turn your face up and open your mouth, and the water drips in, drop by drop.

It's hard to imagine real, desperate thirst, because we can almost always have water when we want it. As you know from experience, sometimes the air gets so full of moisture that water falls right out of the sky. But although we rarely think about it, neither we nor any other form of life on our planet could survive without water.

We learned in the last chapter that almost three-fourths of our planet's surface is covered with water, and 99.99 percent of that is in Earth's oceans. But did you know that the tiny remainder — .01 percent — is just as necessary for our survival as all the rest of it put together? That one-tenth of 1 percent is how much of our planet's water is fresh (nonsalt). It doesn't seem like very much, does it? And it seems like even less if you consider that three-fourths of *that* amount is frozen into the world's glaciers.

Our tiny amount of fresh water is produced by the Earth-ship's own system. Water that is evaporated from the surface of the planet (leaving salt and other impurities behind) eventually falls back down to Earth, where much of it collects in various bodies of fresh water, such as lakes, creeks, rivers, and so on.

Fresh water is what we use at home, in industry, and in irrigated agriculture. Since it's absolutely necessary for our survival, you'd think we'd be very careful with Earth's freshwater supplies. But the sad truth is we aren't. Almost everywhere on the planet, these supplies are shrinking because of waste and misuse; and almost everywhere they are becoming polluted.

FRESH WATER .01%

SALT WATER 99.99%

EARTH'S WATER

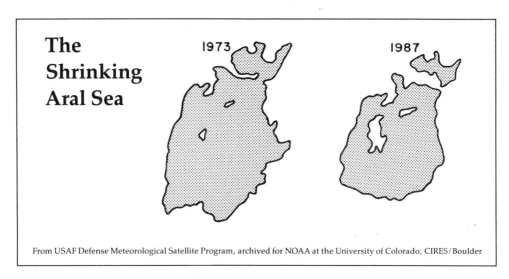

The Shrinking Aral Sea

1973

1987

From USAF Defense Meteorological Satellite Program, archived for NOAA at the University of Colorado, CIRES / Boulder

The map above gives you one startling example of how much one body of water, the Aral Sea in Russia, shrank in less than ten years. Over the last thirty years, its volume has dropped by two-thirds, and it has become three times saltier. All of its native fish species have disappeared. The wind has picked up salt from around its dry bed and carried it to surrounding croplands, where the salt damages crops and even the soil. Saving the Aral Sea has become a top priority in Russia.

As we discussed in the first chapter, there's nothing wrong with using the resources that the Earth-ship's system provides. But problems come up when we take more than we need and waste it, or when our use of a resource either destroys it for future consumption or creates damaging by-products.

Let's take the first problem first: waste. It's hard to think of water as a scarce and precious resource, because it seems so easy to come by. All you have to do is turn a handle, and it comes pouring out of a shiny tube. But just because water comes out of a faucet doesn't mean it's easy to get.

Earth's freshwater supply is constantly replenished by precipitation, but we don't control when, where, or how much of it falls. Many of our cities, especially in the western half of the United States, are built where there is little rain and there are no large bodies of fresh water nearby. So the cities have to move water to where the people are. They use all sorts of methods — from building pipelines to diverting rivers to constructing dams.

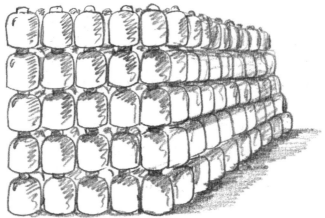

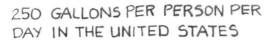

250 GALLONS PER PERSON PER
DAY IN THE UNITED STATES

LESS THAN ONE
GALLON PER PERSON
PER DAY IN KENYA

Often people have no idea how much effort goes into getting their water to them — or how fragile a water supply is. And so we waste water in countless ways. If you live in a large household in the United States, with a big lawn or garden, a dishwasher, and a washing machine, your family might be using as many as 250 gallons of water per person per day. But if you lived in Kenya, where your mother had to walk some distance to haul water, your family might use less than a gallon per person per day.

There's a huge difference between 1 gallon and 250 gallons. One is far too little, but the other is way, way too much.

Fortunately, wasting water is something that each of us can change in our own lives. At the end of this chapter are some activities and suggestions about how to conserve this precious resource.

The other problem with the way we're using Earth's water is that we often contaminate it. There are two major types of human-made pollution that end up in our supplies of fresh water. Industrial waste, produced during various industrial processes, is the more toxic kind. The other kind is traditional organic waste: garbage. Believe it or not, we actually dump both kinds into our own drinking water!

Fortunately for us, pollution of rivers and lakes can be cleaned up, and the processes causing it can be reversed — *if* we get busy and take action. But there's another kind of water, called *groundwater*, that can't be cleaned once it is polluted.

Large quantities of Earth's fresh water exist in hidden places under its surface. Over thousands of years, water has slowly seeped into the earth and accumulated in certain geologic formations (called *aquifers*), where it gets trapped.

But where water seeps into the ground, so can organic and industrial wastes. Leaky sewers, seeping waste dumps, cracked fuel and chemical containers, even toxic chemicals poured down your own kitchen sink — all these and more threaten Earth's groundwater.

In many parts of the world, groundwater is a very important source of drinking water. If you live outside of a city in the United States, you probably get your water from a well that taps into groundwater. Unfortunately, though, a number of wells in several different areas of the country have tested poorly for certain pollutants in recent years. In other words, the water in them is contaminated and no longer safe to drink. Since we are so dependent on groundwater, it is crucial that we do a better job of keeping it clean.

Another problem with groundwater is that it can't be replenished as fast as we're using it. It took thousands of years to collect, but we use it by the billions of gallons without carefully considering what we'll do when we've pumped it all up.

Just one aquifer alone, the Ogallala Aquifer, supplies water to one-fifth of the irrigated cropland in the United States. It is so huge that it lies under parts of eight states in the High Plains region, covering an area about three times as large as the state of New York.

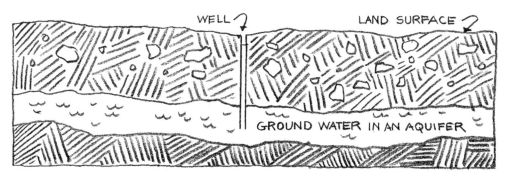

Farmers in Texas, Nebraska, Kansas, Oklahoma, Colorado, and New Mexico have relied on the Ogallala Aquifer to water their crops for nearly fifty years, but the aquifer is quickly being depleted. In fact, water experts (called *hydrologists*) estimate that under parts of Kansas, New Mexico, and Texas it is now half gone!

What do you suppose will happen to the farmers — and all the people who depend on their crops (like you and me) — when the Ogallala Aquifer is pumped dry? It isn't a pleasant thought.

The good news is that new water-saving irrigation technologies are being developed and tested all over the world. The bad news is that governments everywhere make it easy for people to waste water by not charging a price for it that reflects the cost of making it available.

You can see that there are lots of things we need to do to improve the way we use and think about water. Here are some activities that will help you care for Earth's freshwater supply.

— Adopt a Body (of water, that is) —

No matter where you live, there's probably some body of fresh water nearby. And whether it's a lake, a stream, or a river, there's a good chance that it needs your help.

Go for a visit and check it out. What do you see? More than likely, it's trash, trash, and more trash.

If you want to organize a serious cleanup effort, take your idea to a teacher at school and see if it can be turned into a classroom or school project. Here's the story of one successful school project:

Pigeon Creek is a small stream that flows through the city of Everett, Washington. Before it empties into Puget Sound, it runs just below Jackson Elementary School. The students at Jackson saw the creek mostly as a dump, because that's what it had looked like for more than twenty years. But it had once been a clear, clean stream where salmon returned every year to spawn.

When the Jackson principal announced that the school was going to adopt Pigeon Creek, everybody got to work. The kids collected so much trash from the banks of the stream — everything from bottles and cans to old bedsprings — that it took many truckloads to haul it away. They even patrolled the area after school and on weekends to prevent new dumping.

After the cleanup, the school purchased a big aquarium and stocked it with salmon eggs, and the students took turns caring for the tank. Then, when the eggs hatched and the young salmon were finally ready, the kids released them into the creek.

Two years later, some of the salmon that had been raised in the school aquarium began returning to the creek to spawn. Even though many people had said Pigeon Creek was beyond saving, the kids had changed it from a garbage dump into a clear-flowing stream that could support salmon once again.

Every Drip Counts

Here are some simple water-saving tips that you can use and pass on to your friends and family:

- Turn off the water while you brush your teeth, and you'll save up to nine gallons of water every time.

- Save about twenty-five gallons when you wash dishes by filling the sink with soapy water instead of leaving the water running.

- Save up to one hundred gallons of water when you wash the car by turning the hose off except when you're rinsing.

- Save about twenty-five gallons of water by taking short showers instead of baths.

- Sweep sidewalks and driveways with a broom rather than using the hose to clean them.

- Check all the faucets and hoses in and around your house for leaks. A dripping faucet can waste three hundred gallons of water a month.

5

Just Plain Dirt

Did you ever think of soil — just plain dirt — as a fragile part of our Earth system? As a matter of fact, not only is soil part of the big system, it is a system all by itself. It is made of finely ground-up rock from the surface of the earth, chemical elements that are found in the earth's crust, and organic matter, which is the decayed remains of billions of plants, insects, and other animals.

If you look at a picture of a moonscape and compare it to a landscape on Earth, what is the biggest difference you see? The first thing I notice is that there aren't any plants (or any other kinds of life) on the moon. Without life, there can be no soil. Ground-up rock particles can make gravel, sand, or even dust; but without organic matter, rock particles will never become soil.

Wind and water are constantly working on rocks at the earth's surface to break them down into smaller and smaller pieces. The bacteria of decay do a similar job with the remains of plants and animals. But you can imagine that grinding up all that rock, and turning dead plants and animals into organic matter, takes a long, long time.

In fact, one inch of soil takes from two hundred to a thousand years to form, but it can be washed or blown away in just a few years — or even less. Over the entire surface of our planet, 24 billion tons of topsoil are lost every year. This is equal in weight to 4 billion elephants, which is enough elephants to stretch from here to the moon and back twenty times!

There are many reasons for this loss of soil, but they all boil down to one thing: human pressure. If you have only a tiny piece of land where you grow all the food for your family (and that is the case with billions of people all over the world), you are probably going to try to get more out of the land than it is able to give.

First, you might cut down all the trees for firewood, or to make room for crops or grazing animals (you will find out more about this process, called *deforestation*, in the next chapter). Then, after the land has been cleared, you might end up putting more livestock on it than it can support, because this may be your only way of making sure that your family will get enough protein.

If there are too many animals for your small patch of land, they will chew off all the grasses and eventually most of the rest of the vegetation. Once the soil is exposed to wind and weather (the same processes that grind up rock to form soil), it can be blown or washed away.

The same thing happens when land is overused for growing crops. If soil is overused, it becomes depleted (which means that plants can no longer be grown in it). Since the soil is no longer protected by vegetation, it eventually blows or washes away.

The loss of soil (also called *land degradation*) is a serious problem, because — just as there can't be any soil without plants — there can't be any plants without soil. Soil and plants are hitched together so tightly that you can't have one without the other.

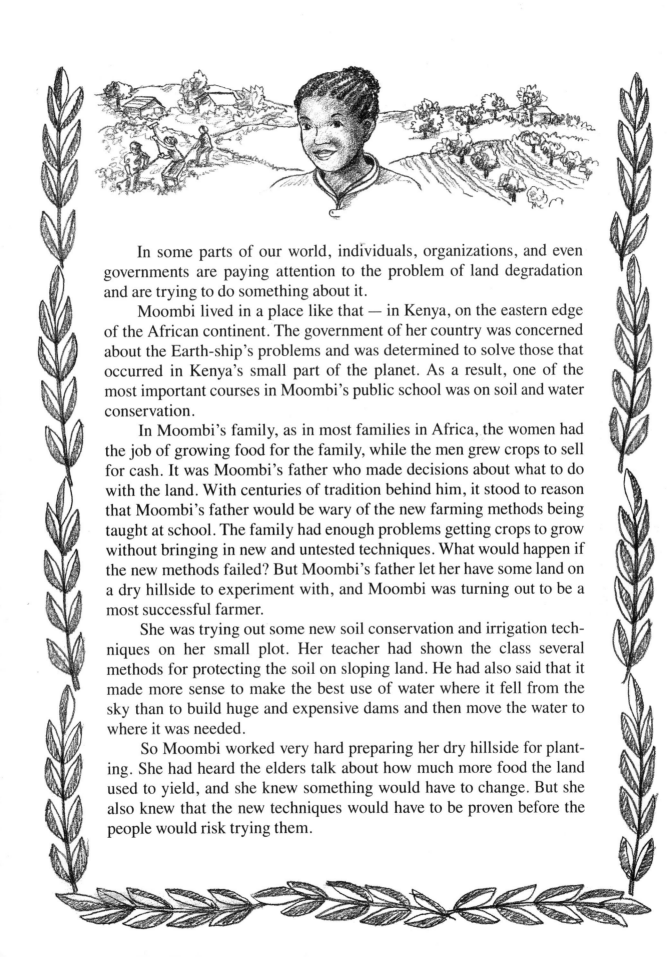

In some parts of our world, individuals, organizations, and even governments are paying attention to the problem of land degradation and are trying to do something about it.

Moombi lived in a place like that — in Kenya, on the eastern edge of the African continent. The government of her country was concerned about the Earth-ship's problems and was determined to solve those that occurred in Kenya's small part of the planet. As a result, one of the most important courses in Moombi's public school was on soil and water conservation.

In Moombi's family, as in most families in Africa, the women had the job of growing food for the family, while the men grew crops to sell for cash. It was Moombi's father who made decisions about what to do with the land. With centuries of tradition behind him, it stood to reason that Moombi's father would be wary of the new farming methods being taught at school. The family had enough problems getting crops to grow without bringing in new and untested techniques. What would happen if the new methods failed? But Moombi's father let her have some land on a dry hillside to experiment with, and Moombi was turning out to be a most successful farmer.

She was trying out some new soil conservation and irrigation techniques on her small plot. Her teacher had shown the class several methods for protecting the soil on sloping land. He had also said that it made more sense to make the best use of water where it fell from the sky than to build huge and expensive dams and then move the water to where it was needed.

So Moombi worked very hard preparing her dry hillside for planting. She had heard the elders talk about how much more food the land used to yield, and she knew something would have to change. But she also knew that the new techniques would have to be proven before the people would risk trying them.

Moombi's mother worked in a tree nursery that was run by the women's Green Belt Movement, and when Moombi explained what she wanted to do, she was given many seedlings of a special type of tree, called a *leucaena*. Moombi's mother told her that these trees had the special ability to fertilize the soil as they grew. They also could be trimmed constantly for fodder to feed animals, and for firewood.

The method Moombi used — planting trees across the face of the hill, among the food crops — was called *alley cropping*. The rows would not only trap soil but capture runoff from the hillside and allow it to seep into the field.

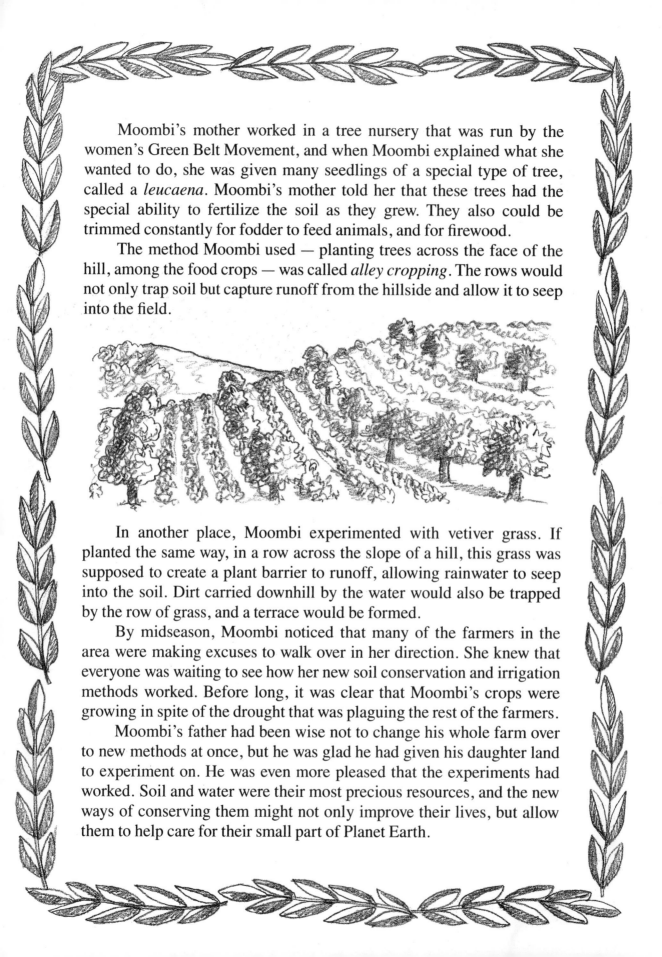

In another place, Moombi experimented with vetiver grass. If planted the same way, in a row across the slope of a hill, this grass was supposed to create a plant barrier to runoff, allowing rainwater to seep into the soil. Dirt carried downhill by the water would also be trapped by the row of grass, and a terrace would be formed.

By midseason, Moombi noticed that many of the farmers in the area were making excuses to walk over in her direction. She knew that everyone was waiting to see how her new soil conservation and irrigation methods worked. Before long, it was clear that Moombi's crops were growing in spite of the drought that was plaguing the rest of the farmers.

Moombi's father had been wise not to change his whole farm over to new methods at once, but he was glad he had given his daughter land to experiment on. He was even more pleased that the experiments had worked. Soil and water were their most precious resources, and the new ways of conserving them might not only improve their lives, but allow them to help care for their small part of Planet Earth.

Here's a soil-related project that you can do to help the Earth-ship in two ways: You'll cut down on the amount of garbage your family throws away, and you'll make rich organic fertilizer to put around trees, bushes, and plants.

Garbage into Soil

Did you know that more than half of the garbage your family throws away could be turned into beautiful, dark, rich soil? It's true. Almost anything that's *organic,* which means that it was once alive, can be turned into soil. This process is called *composting*, and what you end up with at the end of it is *compost*.

All compost piles use the same raw materials: (1) sticks and twigs; (2) kitchen garbage (like ends of carrots, coffee grounds, banana peels, and so on — except for meat); (3) manure; (4) leaves, grass clippings, or weeds from the yard; and (5) water.

The simplest method involves making layers of these things in a pile in your yard or garden. Begin with the sticks and twigs (this will be the only layer of those). Then pile on the kitchen garbage, manure, and yard materials over the sticks and twigs. As you're creating the layers (which may take months), water the pile and pack it down. When the heap gets about four feet high, loosen it up with a pitchfork, cover it with a big, opened-up plastic trash bag, and let it sit for five or six months.

It's easier to build a compost heap if you have some kind of container around it. One way to make a container is to get a length of chicken wire (about nine feet long and four feet high) and make it into a large tube. Use a pair of pliers to fasten the cut ends of the chicken wire together. Up-end the tube in a convenient place in your yard and start building layers inside it. Again, start with a layer of sticks and twigs, and then continue with the other layers until the pile is about four feet high. Keep it moist as you build the layers, and then cover it for five or six months.

No matter which method you use, when you finally remove the plastic, all that smelly garbage and manure will have turned into beautiful soil.

Be-Good-to-Dirt Tips

- One way you can help conserve Earth's soils is to not waste anything that grows in them. Compost leaves and grass clippings, recycle paper (there will be tips in Chapter 11 on how to do that), and don't take more food on your plate than you can eat.

- Many fruits and vegetables are now being grown organically — that is, without chemical fertilizers and pesticides. Talk to your parents about buying organically grown products.

- Since overgrazing stresses soils, and since it takes one-twentieth the raw materials to produce a meal made of vegetables and fruits as it does to produce one with meat, try cutting down on the amount of meat you eat.

6

Forests Are Fundamental

Did you know that the first form of life on Earth was a plant? If we could go back 3 billion years and find that very first plant, we would be meeting a real hero, because without it, life today would not have been possible.

There's one thing plants can do that other life-forms can't: They take carbon dioxide from the atmosphere, light from the sun, and water from the earth and turn them into sugar. This process, called *photosynthesis*, is one of the most important operations on Earth. Not only does it produce food for all other forms of life, but, as it occurs, water molecules are split apart and oxygen is released into the atmosphere. The air you breathe is about 20 percent oxygen, and most of that oxygen was produced by plants through geologic time.

We talked in Chapter 2 about how trees are actually solar storage units, and how if you cut them down you can recover the energy in them. Well, the same thing is true for all the other types of plants. They all store solar energy and, among other things, turn it into food.

All the food you eat is based on plants. Even if you don't eat anything in your life except hamburgers, your diet is still based on plants, because cows eat plants to stay alive and grow.

Because plants grow in such a short time, people realized thousands of years ago that crops could be planted again and again to produce a steady supply of food. Unfortunately for the Earth-ship, people haven't yet realized that the same is true for trees.

What we *are* beginning to realize, though, is that we can't take away one part of the Earth-ship's system without changing, and possibly damaging or destroying, the rest. If we remove the big hardwood trees in a rain forest, for example, the whole rain forest ecosystem is in danger.

The disappearance of tropical rain forests due to human activity is a good example of how ignorance of the Earth-ship's system can cause serious damage. Although tropical rain forests exist in only a narrow strip around the equator and cover less than 2 percent of our planet's surface, they contain more than half of the world's plant and animal species.

One out of every four of the medicines and drugs we use when we're sick is made out of a plant that grows in a rain forest. But rain forest plants not only give us food, medicine, and lumber; they take carbon dioxide out of the atmosphere and put oxygen back into it. The Amazon rain forest, *all by itself*, produces 40 percent of the world's oxygen. Can you imagine what would happen to our planet if we cut all the rain forests down?

World Rain Forests

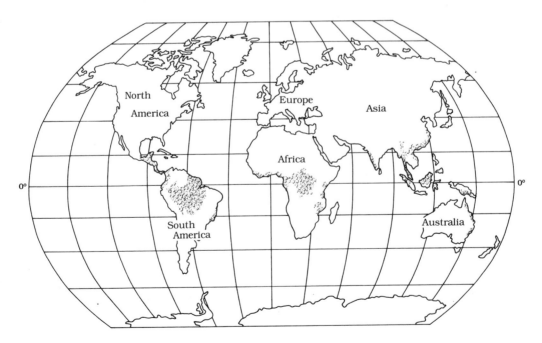

The problem isn't only with rain forests, but with all forests everywhere. Imagine what would happen if we allowed all the trees on Earth to be cut down or killed. The consequences would be terrible. Fortunately, people are beginning to recognize the danger and are figuring out how to avoid it.

Have you ever done something that seemed like a good idea at the time (like eating two hot fudge sundaes in a row) and then wished you hadn't? There's a term that describes a decision that's based on getting something as fast as possible, because we want it *right now*, no matter what the future consequences might be. It's a *short-sighted* decision. And it's these kinds of decisions that are getting us into trouble with our Earth-ship.

We need trees because we can use them for building, or because we can burn them to keep warm and cook our food, or for many other reasons, and so we cut down our forests without making sure they will grow back again. We need more food crops, so we farm or graze animals on land that is fragile and end up destroying the soil.

Even though it might seem strange, severe poverty is one of the greatest threats to the Earth-ship's system, because it causes people to stress the land in many ways. A large part of the population of our planet doesn't flick a switch to get light, or turn a dial to get heat, or push a button to cook food. Instead, these people burn wood as their basic source of energy. Try to imagine how important wood would be if you used it for all those things, and how difficult your life would be without it.

But removing trees from the land damages the Earth-ship, and it's directly related to another serious problem, which we talked about in Chapter 5: soil erosion. When trees are removed from the soil (to provide people with necessities), their roots no longer keep the soil from blowing or washing away. To make things worse, an important source of soil nutrients is removed with the trees. But because people need to grow food, they have to keep using the same depleted soil until, finally, it can no longer produce crops.

Deforestation is a serious problem both in our own country and all over the planet. The rapid clearing of forests — and especially of tropical rain forests — is one of the most damaging things humankind is doing to the Earth-ship. Not only is it destroying the forests themselves, but it is also destroying a way of life for the people and other creatures who live in them.

Marco lived in a tropical rain forest and loved it with a desperation that made him willing to fight for it. As a matter of fact, he was actually engaged in a war for the rain forest, and had been for most of his life. So far the war had robbed him of one cousin (his childhood playmate), one uncle, a man who had been his friend and teacher, and hundreds of thousands of acres of rain forest.

Marco lived on a rubber estate near a small town in the Amazon basin. His country was poor, the economy in tatters, and the government had decided that the Amazon rain forest could provide badly needed money. So it moved both poor settlers and wealthy ranchers into the forest — and acre after acre of trees began to fall.

But the Indians, rubber tappers, and other backwoods people, whose families had been living in the forest and collecting its products for many hundreds of years, had finally been pushed too far. They knew the ways of the forest; they loved and respected it. Finally they decided to fight.

When Marco was a tiny child, he had been in the first battle of this war. His father's friend, Chico Mendez, had begun organizing the local rubber tappers into a union. One day, three rubber tappers came running into town, hot, exhausted, and panic stricken.

One man jerked his thumb back over his shoulder, saying, "They've come . . . there's at least a hundred men with chain saws — and there are gunmen everywhere, guarding them. They've begun clearing the trees."

Chico Mendez and Marco's father had quickly rounded up seventy people from their town — men, women, and children. They all marched together into the forest and, holding hands, stood between the work crew and gunmen and the trees. This first *empate,* or "standoff," worked because the police knew there would be big trouble if they killed women and children.

Since that day, Marco had been in many *empates*, and he knew that he and his people were helping to stop the clearing of the rain forest. Rubber tappers and other forest people throughout the Amazon were beginning to get organized, but they were paying the highest possible price for their efforts.

Chico Mendez had been given a prize by the United Nations for his work in helping to save the Amazon rain forest. Marco, who had known him all his life, knew that Chico deserved the world's highest honors. But the very next year, Chico was dead — killed by gunmen who wanted to stop his work.

The probability of violence against his own family had been part of Marco's reality since he was a small boy. The death of his friend and teacher, Chico, had left a wound that would never heal, and he lived in fear of a gun blast aimed at his own father. He also knew that if he continued in this work, if he followed in his father's footsteps, his own life could be a short one.

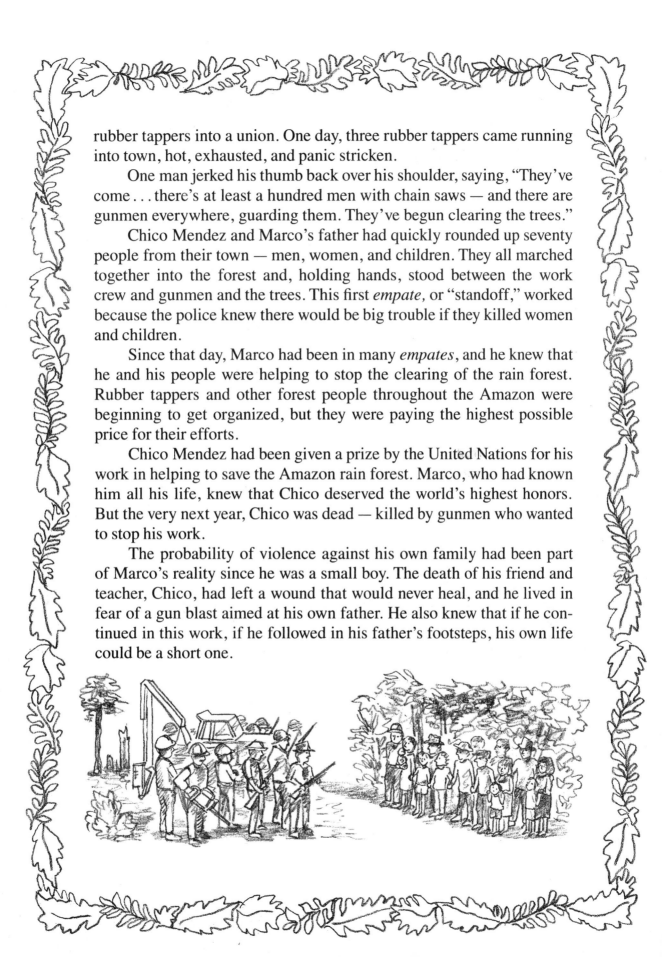

But today was a new day, and it marked a special rite of passage for Marco. Although he was only sixteen, he had been given the job of organizing an *empate* by himself. It had taken him more than a month, but it was going to be a very big *empate*. Marco had gathered more than a hundred people: members of the Rural Workers Unions from as far as 250 miles away, and forest people from all over his state. Most of them had come on foot, over rivers and impossible roads through the rain forest.

Marco had set up the *mutirao* ("gathering place") a little more than half a mile from the gunmen's camp. It was just barely dawn, and they would begin to march in an hour. Marco stood in the forest and let the green dawn wash over him. The birds were already busy, calling to each other in a hundred voices. Marco knew that what he was doing was right. The people that were gathered together were unarmed except for their working machetes and axes, and that was how it should be — even though they were marching against heavily armed men.

Marco had been through this countless times before, but his stomach was still knotted in fear. The fear was so familiar that Marco didn't worry about it any more. He knew that once he started marching it would go away. He took one last look at the forest and then walked back through the trees to begin the *empate*.

Although Marco's work to save the Earth-ship put him in danger, most of us can practice planet care and repair in relative comfort and safety. One thing we can all do is try to understand some of the processes that create stress on Earth's systems. One of these is the unequal distribution of the world's wealth. This game will help you understand how that works.

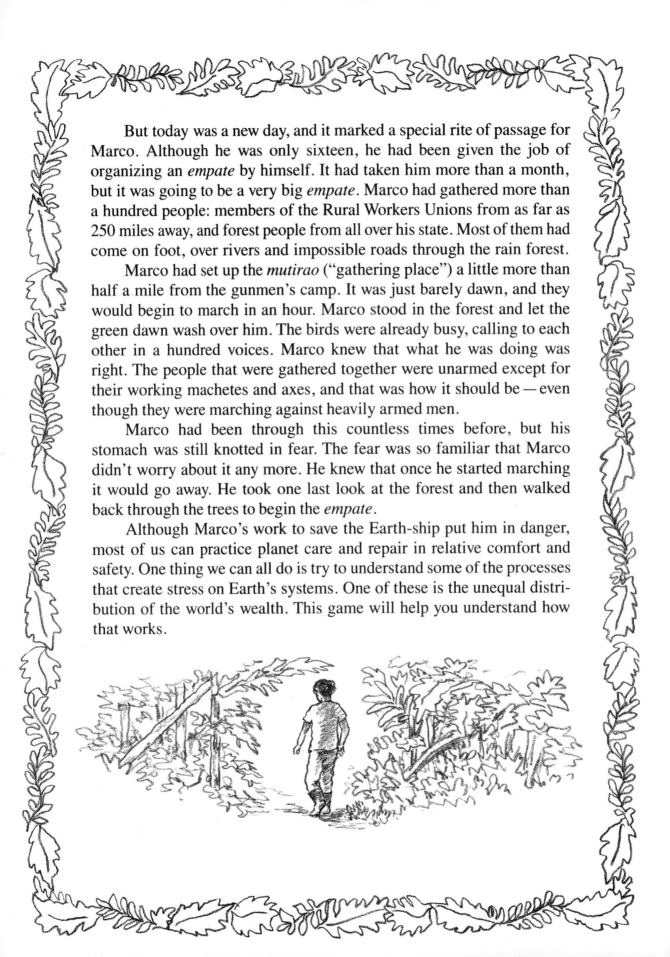

Shares

Although it would be nice if everybody on the planet had enough of the world's resources to live happily and safely, that just isn't the way it works. This game will help you understand how goods and money are distributed around the world, and it might give you an idea of why poverty causes people to overuse some of the basic resources of our planet.

To play Shares, you will need five people. One person will be the arbitrator, and the other four will be citizens of four different countries. (If you have only four people, you can probably get along without an arbitrator.)

You'll need quite a few supplies to play Shares, but most are things you normally have around the house. You'll need some nuts, raisins, or M&M's; some colored pencils, markers, or crayons; two regular pencils; one clean sheet of paper; one paper bag; one piece of scrap paper (like the back of an envelope) from the trash; one sheet of newspaper; and a clock or watch.

The game will show you how average income (represented by nuts, raisins, or M&M's), life expectancy (represented by minutes of playing time), and availability of commercial products (represented by drawing materials) compare among four different countries: the United States, Portugal, Nicaragua, and Ethiopia.

Before the game begins, write the name of each of these countries on a separate piece of paper. Fold the papers so that they all look alike, and put them in a dish. The four players will close their eyes and, one at a time, pick one of the pieces of paper. Each player will then be a citizen of the country that she or he selected.

The arbitrator will divide and distribute the food shares in proportion to the average income per person in each country: The person in the United States gets 40 nuts, raisins, or M&M's; in Portugal, 8; in Nicaragua, 2; and in Ethiopia, ½. (You can eat the food shares or give them away. If your allotment is small, ask someone who has more to give you some.)

The average life expectancy (that is, how long the average person can expect to live) has been calculated for each country and translated into minutes of playing time. The person in the United States gets 12

minutes; in Portugal, 11 minutes; in Nicaragua, 9 minutes; and in Ethiopia, 7 minutes.

The task of the game is for each player to make a self-portrait in the time allotted, using the materials provided according to the economic conditions in her or his country. The arbitrator will use the clock to begin the game and to time the "life," in minutes, of each person who is playing.

The person from the United States will use the clean sheet of paper and any kind of colored pencils, markers, or crayons. The person from Portugal will use the side of a paper bag and a pencil. The person from Nicaragua will use a pencil and a piece of scrap paper from the trash. The person from Ethiopia receives nothing to write with, so she or he must tear, fold, or in some other way use the newspaper to make a self-portrait.

The materials in this game aren't necessarily typical of things you'd find in the countries they're supposed to represent. They are just ways of indicating the different economic conditions in the four countries.

Once all the materials have been distributed, the arbitrator can start the game. Seven minutes later, the Ethiopian must stop; nine minutes after the beginning, the Nicaraguan must stop; and so on.

After you have finished your self-portraits, you can share them with the other players and talk about how it felt to play the game in the role you selected at the beginning.

KEEP WATER COVERING 1/3 OF SEED.

FOR BEST RESULTS, USE A SEED FROM AN AVOCADO THAT WAS NEVER REFRIGERATED

Grow a Tree

Did you know that the average tree consumes around thirteen pounds of carbon dioxide a year? If a hundred thousand people planted trees this year, those trees would be absorbing more than a million pounds of carbon dioxide annually by the year 2010.

If you would like to participate in this kind of global air cleanup, try planting a tree. Sometimes you can buy tiny saplings for very little money at a tree nursery. The people at the nursery can help you choose a tree that would be best for your area, and they can tell you exactly how to plant and take care of it. Plant nurseries often have illustrated instruction sheets to help you with the planting.

If you don't want to spend money on this project, you can grow a tree from a seed. One of the easiest seeds to grow comes out of an avocado, which is used to make guacamole. All you need is the seed, some toothpicks, and a glass or jar.

Put the toothpicks in the seed, and the seed on the glass, as shown in the picture above. Fill the glass with water so that the bottom third of the seed is immersed. Then put the glass on a sunny windowsill. Check the water every day to be sure the bottom of the seed is always immersed.

After the seed has sprouted and the tree is several inches high, you can plant it in some dirt. (Unless you live in a warm climate with mild winters, your tree will have to grow in a pot in your house.) When you plant it, make a hole in the dirt and carefully bury the seed with the small tree sticking out of the soil.

7

Wildlife in Danger

Have you ever looked at a tiny opening in a cliffside, or a little space under a tree root, and imagined it would be an interesting place to live if you were only one inch tall? The great thing is that there probably *is* something one inch tall living there!

Our planet has all kinds of places for creatures to live. There are tiny nooks and crannies, and huge wide open spaces; there are oceans more than two miles deep, and deserts that cover millions of square miles. And each of these places provides a home for some of Earth's creatures.

Every living thing on Earth has its own special place where it lives out its life. That place is called its *habitat*. Some plants and animals have very specific habitats, and they can't survive anyplace else. Koala bears, for instance, live only where a certain type of eucalyptus tree grows, and that happens to be only in Australia. Human beings, on the other hand, have learned to live in almost any environment. Next to people, house-flies are the most far-ranging species.

The interesting thing about habitats and the creatures that live in them is that they develop and change together. In fact, many creatures actually blend in with their habitat. A polar bear is white and very hard to see against snow and ice. A red-and-gold parrot is as bright as it can be, but in its jungle home, it looks like just another flower.

If you put a polar bear in the jungle or a parrot on an ice floe, though, each one would stand out like a neon sign in the other's environment. Not only would they look out of place, but they wouldn't have anything to eat or any way to protect themselves from the strange weather.

Polar bears, for example, live only where three certain conditions exist: They need cold water, seafood (mostly seals), and drift ice. If any one of these things is missing, polar bears can't survive. Parrots, on the other hand, have adapted to their jungle habitat so perfectly that they have a tool on their heads specifically made to crack open tropical nuts with hard shells. (It's their beak!)

Since polar bears and parrots both developed in their own habitats, at the same time the habitats themselves were developing, the creatures and their environments are in perfect harmony. You can imagine, then, that if something happens to damage (or destroy) a habitat, all of the creatures who live in it are in serious trouble. Unfortunately, that is exactly what's happening all over the world today.

Sometimes the trouble is so extreme that entire populations of animals are unable to survive. When all the members of a certain species die, that species becomes *extinct*. If you have a hard time imagining what that means, here is an example:

What if there was such a devastating catastrophe that almost all the people on Earth died, and you turned out to be the very last human being on the planet? Even if you lived to be one hundred and four, after you died, there would never be another human. That is what extinction means: Once something is extinct, it is gone forever.

Extinction is a *natural* process; in fact, all species will eventually become extinct. The average natural rate of extinction is about ten species per year. But, unfortunately, one species — and I'm sorry to say that you and I belong to it — has multiplied that rate several thousand times! In other words, we humans are causing the kinds of catastrophes all over the planet that are serious enough to wipe out entire species.

There are several stages on the road to extinction. First, a species is classified as *threatened,* which means that if the processes that have put it at risk are not reversed, it may become extinct. At the next stage, it becomes *endangered,* which means that it is in imminent danger of extinction. Sadly, we have watched thousands of species move through these stages; many of them, like the passenger pigeon, have gone right to the end and have disappeared from Earth forever.

One of the major ways that humans speed up the rate of extinction is through the destruction of habitats. Our rapid destruction of Earth's tropical rain forests is a good example. Worldwide, these very special, amazingly rich ecosystems have been reduced to less than half their original size. In the Amazon rain forest, 80 percent of the total deforestation has happened since 1980. Since creatures are tied to their habitats, this destruction has had devastating results. One biologist estimates that almost 140 rain forest species are condemned to extinction every day!

Even many species of primates (the order we humans belong to, along with monkeys and lemurs) are threatened by habitat loss. Of the world's 200 species of primates, 116 are threatened with extinction.

The other major way humans cause species extinction is through hunting. Interestingly, some of the biggest creatures on Earth have been the most profitable targets for hunters. In fact, whole industries have

been built around the hunting and killing of Earth's largest animals. Whales are a good example. We began hunting them in the days of wooden sailing ships and hand-thrown harpoons. We still hunt them today, but now we use high technology for finding and killing these huge mammals. As one species of whale has gotten depleted, we've moved on to the next.

The good news is that the International Whaling Commission banned commercial whaling in 1986, and since then, the killing of whales all over the world has dropped dramatically. The bad news is that Norway recently announced its plan to start hunting minke whales again, and Iceland has quit the International Whaling Commission. Japan also wants minke hunting reopened. Will these creatures survive?

Another large animal that has been hunted into the endangered category is the elephant. Here's a riddle for you: What do old-time piano keys, dice, and certain pieces of jewelry have in common? The answer is, they're all made out of ivory — or, in other words, elephant tusks. That is, they *used* to be made out of ivory.

In 1990, more than a hundred countries signed the Convention on Trade in Endangered Species, which outlaws trade involving any species threatened with extinction. Within months, the world ivory market dried up. Poaching (illegal hunting) fell from a kill of seventy thousand elephants per year to fourteen thousand per year.

Whales and elephants are hard to miss, and when people began to realize that these gigantic creatures might disappear forever, they started boycotting products, writing letters, forming organizations, and generally making a big stink about it. Their efforts paid off, and whales and elephants are now legally protected. (The project at the end of this chapter will show you how *you* can influence legal decisions, too.) Unfortunately, tiny creatures, such as snails or bugs, rarely receive that kind of attention.

But being small isn't the same as being unimportant. For one thing, each species of plant or animal — whether it's tiny or huge — represents a unique form of life, and one that's taken many thousands of years to develop. For another, each one is an important part of its own ecosystem, and if it becomes extinct, the whole system may be thrown out of balance.

As you have seen, people can do many things to prevent such disasters. Here is a story about a girl who found a way to help out some of her favorite creatures:

Billie Ruth lived in southern Florida, near a small river called Fish Eating Creek. She was the youngest kid in a big family, and she had spent much of her life out on the creek with various combinations of brothers and sisters.

Early summer was Billie Ruth's favorite time of year. It was the rainy season, which meant rain every afternoon, but it also meant that the creek was in its tropical jungle mode. Everything was green, except for the flowers and the birds, and they came in all sorts of amazing colors. Best of all, it was playtime for the animals.

So Billie Ruth spent every day out on the creek. One morning she made a lunch and took her family's small boat out to spy on a family of river otters that usually got playful in the early afternoon. She anchored the boat in her favorite place, where branches from trees on each side of the creek met high overhead to form a complete canopy over the water. She made a nest out of the boat's life vests and cushions, hung her binoculars around her neck, got a drumstick and two oranges out of her pack, and sat back to watch the show.

While she was waiting for the otters to appear, she heard a funny, high-pitched squealing sound. At first she thought it was a bird of some sort — but she had never heard a bird that sounded quite like that. When it happened again, Billie Ruth realized that the sound was coming from the water somewhere near her boat.

She searched the shallows and finally saw something move. When it moved again, she understood why it had been so hard to find. The huge, gray shape, half in and half out of the river, blended almost perfectly with the water and the shoreline vegetation. It would have been nearly invisible, except that there was a much smaller gray shape moving around it. Billie realized that she was seeing a mother manatee and her baby — and that there was something wrong with the mother.

She had seen manatees hundreds of times on the creek and had a special love for the huge, elephantlike water creatures. They were so funny looking — like gigantic, wrinkled seals with trunklike noses — but they were also the gentlest animals on the creek.

Although she had been around wild creatures all her life and had no fear of them, Billie knew better than to go near an animal with young. She also knew better than to approach an injured animal, especially if it happened to be ten feet long and weigh more than two thousand pounds.

When she fastened her binoculars on the huge creature, there was no doubt that it was badly injured. Billie saw a long gash that went from above its front, flipperlike forelimb clear down to where its torpedo-shaped body was submerged in the water. She guessed that the wound had been made by a boat propeller when the manatee had come to the surface for air. Unfortunately, it was an all-too-common problem.

Billie Ruth was torn between not wanting to leave the hurt animal and her baby alone, and going back to the house to phone for help. She knew there was a manatee hot line to call for just this type of emergency, and she decided that the best thing to do was to go and call it.

She paddled the boat out to the middle of the creek so its motor wouldn't scare the injured animal, and then she started for home. She felt angry at the circumstances that had caused this problem. No one knew how many manatees there had been before the human population explosion in Florida, but there were only about twelve hundred manatees left.

The huge, gentle mammals were at risk of extinction because of human-related problems: loss of habitat, accidents with boats, swallowing of fish hooks and lines, entanglement in crab trap lines, and so on. Seeing the injured manatee and her baby focused all of Billie Ruth's feelings about the wildlife of Fish Eating Creek, and she decided to do something about saving it.

Billie called the manatee hot line as soon as she got home. The person who answered told her he would send out a truck, a boat, and a crew, and he asked Billie to wait for them at her house so she could help them find the injured manatee.

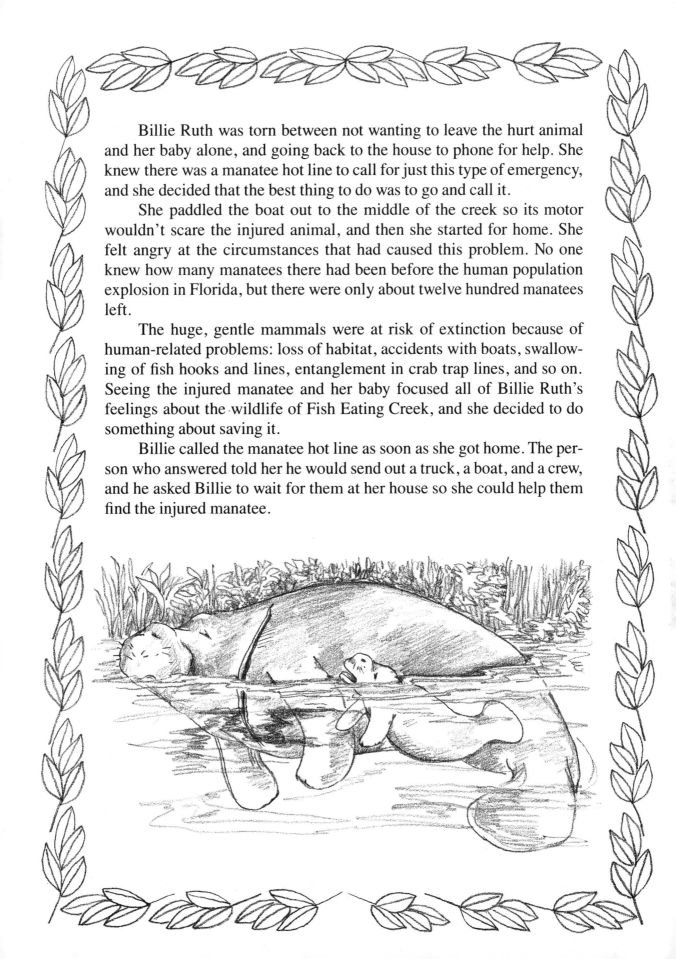

When the rescue crew arrived, Billie Ruth took them up the creek in her own boat, and they towed another strange-looking boat behind them. Billie was worried about finding the manatee and her baby, but they were just where she had left them. She watched in fascination as the special boat was partially sunk in the water near the injured animal, and the crew gently captured the big manatee in a net and rolled her into the boat. In spite of its obvious fear, the baby finally followed its mother into the partially sunken boat, and both animals were secured.

After both boats returned to Billie's house, the crew backed the truck up to the river and used a hydraulic lift and canvas sling to lift the mother and her baby into a special tank in the back of the truck. The whole procedure was very complicated, but the handlers were experts, and several hours after Billie first found them, the manatees were on their way to a special treatment center. If the mother and baby survived (a manatee baby can't live without its mother until it is a year and a half old), they would eventually be sent to live in the Homosassa Springs Wildlife Park.

Billie followed through on her vow to help the manatees by starting a branch of the Save the Manatees Club in her school. She organized her friends to write letters of support for a law that would require all boats to put screens on their propellers (like the one her oldest brother, Jack, had made for their own boat). She also volunteered to help post speed limit signs in the local creeks and rivers.

Billie Ruth's love for her own little creek inspired her to go to work for the creatures that lived there. If you would like to influence major decisions that help protect the Earth-ship and its creatures, here is something you can easily do.

— The Power of the Written Word —

One of the best things you can do to help care for and repair our damaged planet is to let people who make decisions know how you feel about environmental issues. You might be surprised at how much difference a letter can make. Because they are elected by voters (and you're going to be one of those someday), political representatives pay attention to what people say. So do business people and industrial managers.

Here are the addresses of some people who make important decisions:

- President _____ . The White House, Washington, DC 20510
- Senator _____ . U.S. Senate, Washington, DC 20510
- Representative _____ . U.S. House of Representatives, Washington, DC 20515.

You can also send a letter to a representative of a foreign government by writing to that government's embassy at the United Nations, United Nations Plaza, New York, NY 10017.

If you'd like to carry this project further, you can take it to your school or any other group and get lots of other kids involved. Writing letters is one way to make your own small voice heard, and it gives you a way to put your best efforts to work for the Earth-ship.

8

The Ocean of Air

Did you know that you're living beneath an ocean of air? It's deeper than any other ocean on our planet, but since you're too heavy to swim in it, you just wade around on the bottom. This ocean is called the atmosphere, and it's one of the most important parts of the Earth-ship's life support system.

Like any ocean, the atmosphere has waves and currents, and it's full of particles that float around in it and are carried from place to place on those currents. The ocean of air is almost two hundred miles deep, and it covers Earth in many layers, like an onion skin covers an onion.

We're so used to being in this ocean that we usually forget it's there. In fact, it's hard to believe that it forms an almost impenetrable barrier all around our planet. But space scientists found out just how hard it is to get something past it.

In the late 1960s, scientists were working on getting astronauts and their space vehicles safely back to the surface of Earth. The *Apollo* spacecraft re-entered at greater speeds than usual because they did not have retro-rockets to slow them down. The scientists learned that if such a vehicle hit the atmosphere at too shallow an angle, it would bounce back up into space. And if it re-entered at too steep an angle, it would burn up from friction with the atmosphere. Eventually they discovered that a vehicle could only re-enter within two degrees of the optimum re-entry angle, which is six degrees.

You can imagine that the atmosphere works the same way when anything else from space is heading for Earth. It covers our entire planet like a blanket, both regulating the temperature and keeping other pesky things (like meteors) from coming under the covers with us. But it also serves us in many other ways.

For instance, without the atmosphere, there would be no weather. Some parts of the planet would burn to a crisp, and other parts would freeze solid — and none of it would get any rain. The atmosphere also filters out some of the sun's damaging rays and makes the surface of Earth a safe place to live. And, of course, the atmosphere provides us with the air we breathe.

We've really only begun to understand the atmosphere since we figured out a way to see it from a distance. The view from space showed us that the atmosphere is one whole, interconnected system, and that what happens in one small area will eventually spread into the rest of it.

The constant churning of the atmosphere makes the air above us into a global stew. In fact, every time you breathe, you suck in molecules from every corner of the world. But that also means that when you dump something into the atmosphere, it doesn't go away but just keeps spreading.

Up to now, humankind has been pretty careless with our planet's ocean of air. Since it was such a huge ocean, it seemed like a few smokestacks here and there, and a few cars, wouldn't make that much difference. But that turned out to be short-sighted thinking. These days we are dumping millions of tons of nasty substances into the atmosphere every year. And where do they all go? You guessed it: nowhere!

Unfortunately, some of the substances we dump drift to the upper atmosphere, where they produce strange chemical reactions in the ozone layer, which is one of the most important parts of the ocean of air. The ozone layer filters out ultraviolet radiation, a type of solar energy that is harmful to living things. In that way, the ozone layer is directly responsible for making the surface of Earth inhabitable.

But certain chemicals produced in industrial processes actually eat ozone in the upper atmosphere. The process used to manufacture polystyrene is one of the worst culprits. Maybe you've heard that some companies (including some fast-food restaurants) are phasing out polystyrene containers. That's an example of how public pressure can convince businesses to pay more attention to the needs of our Earth-ship.

If you live in a big city, you probably know firsthand about ground-level air pollution. It looks awful, smells worse, and damages everything it touches. Even if you live out in the country, you most likely still experience air pollution — though it may be more indirectly (as in acid rain, which you'll find out about in Chapter 10).

Pollution is an unfortunate by-product of many things that we do every day. Most of our transportation, energy, and industrial systems depend on the burning of fossil fuels to produce their end results. And since combustion of fossil fuels is the chief cause of air pollution (in the form of carbon dioxide), each of us is almost constantly contributing to the problem without even thinking about it.

Another major contributor to the buildup of carbon dioxide in the atmosphere is deforestation. That's because trees take carbon dioxide out of the air and store it as wood; then, when they are cut down, carbon is released back into the atmosphere, either through natural processes of decay or through burning of the wood.

Cutting down trees not only releases carbon, but obviously also eliminates some of the big plants that breathe in carbon dioxide and breathe out oxygen (which is the opposite of the way we animals do it). So saving trees by recycling paper and cutting down on waste also helps the atmosphere.

Throughout the world, all sorts of laws have been passed to clean up the air, but the problem is deeper than that. The problem is that human travelers on the Earth-ship (including you and me, I'm sorry to say) are doing things without paying attention to the consequences of their actions. It's easier to ride in a car than to take the bus or ride a bike. It's easier to leave lights on than to turn them off. And it's easier for manufacturers to make things the same old way than to redesign products and technologies to reduce air pollution.

Someday you and your friends are going to be the decision makers of this world. But even before then, there are things you can do to help solve the pollution problem. One is to write letters to the people who make decisions today. Another is to boycott certain products that either are offensive themselves or are produced in a way that's harmful to the Earth-ship.

A boycott happens when a person (or, more likely, a group of people) refuses to deal with a particular organization or product. The following story is about a boycott.

Two sisters named Brett and Lake found out about polystyrene and its terrible effect on the ozone layer. They decided to start a boycott of all the fast-food and other carry-out restaurants in their town that sold food in polystyrene containers.

That took some effort, because, first of all, they had to call or visit all the restaurants and find out how they packaged food. They also wanted to explain to the owners or managers what they were planning, and to ask them to switch to another type of packaging. Brett and Lake went through the phone book, divided the restaurants, and then either

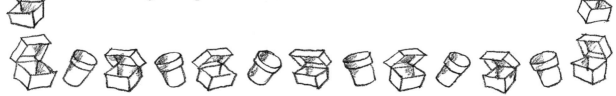

called or paid a visit to each restaurant on their bikes. They were able to cross a few restaurants off their list when the owners agreed to stop using polystyrene. When they were done, they told their parents that there were certain restaurants in town that they were boycotting.

Then Lake and Brett took it a step further. They made a beautiful map of their town and put all the restaurants on it. They used a special symbol to show which restaurants were polystyrene free, and in fancy letters across the top, they printed "SAVE THE OZONE LAYER."

Brett and Lake made copies of the map, colored each one by hand, and put them up all over school. But then they realized that the boycott wouldn't work unless the restaurants remembered what they were doing. So they sent copies of the map to all the restaurants that were still using polystyrene, along with a letter explaining the boycott.

More and more kids at Brett and Lake's school decided to join the boycott. And soon the map spread to other schools in the area, as well. Before long, one restaurant announced that it was banning the use of polystyrene, and then another followed the example.

Lake and Brett knew for sure that their boycott had forced this decision. They and all the other kids involved were very happy — and a little amazed — at the results. Actually, it *is* astounding how much power each of us really has.

If you would like to get involved in planet care and repair by starting a boycott, here are some tips:

——— Do-It-Yourself Boycott ———

The first thing to decide is what sort of product to boycott. Here are a few ideas:

- Any products that come from animals on the endangered species list (jewelry made of ivory, coral, or tortoise shell; skins of certain reptiles; certain animal furs; and so on).

- Anything made of tropical hardwoods.

- Products that are packaged in useless, wasteful containers. (Avoiding such products is called *precycling*. You'll find out more about that in Chapter 11.)

- Restaurants that serve foods that come from endangered animals (like turtle eggs) or that use products that damage the environment (like polystyrene cups and containers).

The next step is to decide whether your boycott is going to be your own personal affair, or whether it's going to be like Brett and Lake's boycott, which involved organizing a group.

Either way, you need to let the businesses you plan to boycott know what you're doing and why, and ask them to change their antienvironmental practices. If they don't respond, the last step is to begin the boycott and send out letters to explain your actions.

9

A Global Greenhouse

Have you ever been sitting right in front of a sunny window on a cold day and had to get up and move because you were too hot? Even if it's very cold *outside*, the combination of direct sunlight and glass will heat the area on the *inside* of a window every time.

What you experienced in front of the sunny window is the same process that makes a greenhouse work. You might have heard of this process lately because it has given its name to one of the most serious threats from air pollution: the *greenhouse effect*.

Here's how the process works: All objects in the universe that possess heat, whether they're big or small, emit a form of energy called *electromagnetic radiation*. This energy travels outward in the form of waves. If the object emitting it is extremely hot, the energy travels in shorter wavelengths; if it is cool, the energy travels in longer wavelengths.

Because the sun is so hot, most of the radiation it emits travels in short wavelengths. As the radiation reaches Earth, some of it hits the atmosphere and bounces off, and some of it is absorbed by the atmosphere. Only about one-fourth of the incoming solar radiation reaches Earth's surface directly. (Another fourth — the part that was absorbed by the atmosphere — reaches Earth indirectly.)

So our planet receives the sun's energy but then radiates it back into space. (That's a good thing, because if it didn't return the sun's energy to space, the planet would burn up.) But because Earth is much colder than the sun, the energy it returns to space travels in longer wavelengths.

The difference in the wavelengths causes the greenhouse effect. A greenhouse is made mostly of glass, which has the property of allowing shortwave radiation to pass right through it. So energy from the sun comes in to provide heat and light for the plants growing inside. But when that energy is converted to longer wavelengths, the glass prevents it from passing out again, so energy (in the form of heat) is trapped inside the greenhouse.

In our atmosphere, there are certain substances that act like glass. These substances (including carbon dioxide, which is a natural component of the atmosphere) are called *greenhouse gases*. They allow shortwave radiation from the sun to pass through, but they keep the longer wavelengths that bounce back from Earth trapped inside. Most scientists agree that this process will create gradual warming of Earth's system, a process that they refer to as *global warming*.

Because carbon dioxide is one of the greenhouse gases, you can see that the burning of fossil fuels contributes in a major way to the greenhouse effect. There is only a tiny amount of carbon dioxide in the atmosphere naturally, but since the Industrial Revolution it has increased by more than 25 percent.

Carbon is one of the biggest waste products in the modern world. And every ton of carbon that is put into the air produces (after it mixes with the atmosphere) more than 3½ tons of carbon dioxide. Recently, various human activities have produced more than *6 billion tons* of carbon every year — and that adds up to more than a ton a year for each human being on Earth.

Now you might be thinking that you, yourself, didn't produce a single bit of carbon last year (at least not that you can remember). But the sad truth is that you actually caused more than *five tons* of it to be produced! That is, if you live in the United States. If you lived in Zaire, Africa, you caused only a tiny fraction of a ton to be produced. The main reason people in Zaire produce so much less carbon than people in the

United States is that the United States is an *energy-intensive* country: People here use much, much more energy than the majority of the people on the planet. For instance, very few people in a country like Zaire have cars, but as we learned in Chapter 2, there are almost enough cars in the United States for every single person to have one of her or his own. And all those cars, of course, have a devastating effect on the Earth-ship's system.

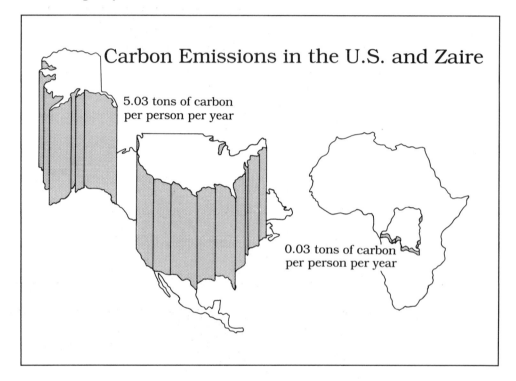

Carbon Emissions in the U.S. and Zaire

5.03 tons of carbon per person per year

0.03 tons of carbon per person per year

It's the short-sighted decision again. And part of what's too bad about it is that, although some countries are contributing much more than others to the problem, the rest of the world suffers equally from the consequences.

Although scientists agree that we are changing the composition of our atmospheric blanket, they have different ideas about what the results will be, or rather, *when* they will be. For instance, the 1980s was the warmest decade on record, with 1988, 1987, and 1981 being the warmest years ever. Some scientists say that is due to greenhouse warming; others say it is too soon to know for sure.

Two of the most agreed-on predictions for the future are that global warming will cause a rise in sea level all over the world and that it will cause a shrinking of croplands. That means that many coastal areas, including some of our biggest cities, may be flooded, and our food supply may be threatened.

But the news isn't all bad. Many people, organizations, and governments are taking steps toward reducing emissions of carbon. Some of these steps involve finding alternative sources of energy; others involve conserving energy or finding more efficient ways to use it.

So far, our own government has lagged behind many others in energy issues. But you now know that your opinion, expressed in letters to representatives of our government, can make a difference. Another thing that you can do is to watch the way you and your family use energy. Small changes — person by person, family by family — add up to big ones.

Here are some tips to help you and your friends and family make a difference.

Energy Tips

- Park the car. Talk to your family about leaving the family car (or cars) parked for one day. You might volunteer to run errands that day on your bike or on foot, and encourage other members of your family to try alternative forms of transportation. If it works, suggest having a park-the-car day at least once a month.

- Check to see that the thermostat in your house is turned no higher than 68 degrees Fahrenheit in the winter and no lower than 78 in the summer. (You can always add or subtract layers of clothing if you're too cool or warm.)

- Turn off unnecessary lights.

- Keep the refrigerator door closed as much as possible. Decide what you want before you open it, and then get it out quickly.

- Insulate your water heater. Most hardware stores have insulated covers made to fit standard water heaters.

10

Brown Air and Acid Rain

Did you know that the word *smog* is a twentieth-century invention? It's a combination of *smoke* and *fog,* and it sounds just like what it is. It sounds heavy. And brown. And when you say it, you can tell that it smells.

The reason somebody had to make up a word like that is because when the rest of the language was invented, heavy, brown, smelly air didn't exist. Smoke was the stuff that came from burning wood, and fog was a large mass of water vapor condensed into tiny droplets.

But now smoke is full of chemicals, and even the water vapor in our air has become polluted. Among other things, it combines with certain by-products of industrial, transportation, and energy-generating systems to become what is referred to as *acid rain.*

Acid rain, like the hole in the ozone layer, happens because of chemical reactions in the atmosphere. These chemical reactions involve common pollutants that are produced by the burning of fossil fuels. Generating electricity by burning coal is the biggest source of these pollutants in today's world. (After coal, automobiles and heavy industries are the biggest producers of the chemicals that create acid rain.)

The major chemical culprits are sulfur dioxide and nitrogen oxides. These gases combine with others in the atmosphere to form sulfuric acid

and nitric acid, which easily dissolve in water. They build up in fog near the ground, or in water vapor in the atmosphere, which eventually falls as rain, snow, sleet, or hail.

You can probably imagine that a solution of sulfuric acid falling on plants, or in lakes, rivers, and streams, does a certain amount of damage. If you do the experiment on the next page, you will find out just what effect a solution of acid in water has on plants. But besides affecting green growing things, acid rain that ends up in bodies of water damages or kills the creatures that live in them.

Although people have been working for years to figure out how to take care of air pollution, some solutions have just created different problems. For instance, tall smokestacks, built to improve the quality of air near the ground, turned out to be the wrong kind of solution. Even though they reduce pollution at ground level, these taller stacks inject the pollutants directly into the atmosphere, where they combine with other gases to form acid precipitation.

The most obvious thing we can do about any kind of air pollution is to change, in small ways, the way we live. We don't have to throw away our cars, or stop using electricity, or get rid of all our high-tech gizmos, but we do need to be more careful about how we design and use them. Who knows? Maybe someday you'll invent a car that runs on Ping-Pong energy and doesn't produce any pollution at all.

Acid Rain Experiment

The most acidic rain ever measured had about as much acid in it as lemon juice. This experiment will show you firsthand how an acidic solution affects growing things.

You will need two small houseplants, and one of them will probably be a sacrifice. It's best to use two plants of the same type. You will also need masking tape, a marking pen, lemon juice, and water.

Write "tap water" on a strip of masking tape, and put it around one of the plant pots. Write "lemon juice" on another strip, and put it around the other pot. Put both plants in a sunny place in your house.

Every two to four days, depending on the type of plant and the climate you live in, the soil in the pots will get dry. When you water the plants, give the tap-water plant regular water and the lemon-juice plant lemon juice.

If you really want to get serious, you can also spray the plants every few days using a spray bottle. The tap-water plant, of course, will get sprayed with water, and the lemon-juice plant will get sprayed with lemon juice (move it to the sink to spray it, or you'll get sticky lemon juice all over everything).

How long does it take before the lemon-juice plant starts showing signs of distress? What is the difference in the way the two plants look after the lemon-juice plant starts to get sick? If you want to, you can try to make the lemon-juice plant better again by watering and spraying it with plain water. Will it survive?

11

All That Garbage

There's something you should know about all that stuff you and your family throw away, and that is *there's no "away" about it!* We load garbage onto barges and dump it in the ocean, we bury it in the ground in "landfills," we ship it to other countries where we don't have to look at it — but it doesn't go away.

Using the ocean as a dump didn't matter quite as much when there were fewer people and when garbage was all organic. But as we learned in Chapter 3, the world's oceans are now having trouble absorbing humanity's waste products. Much of the waste that ends up in the ocean today is toxic (and don't forget, that word means poisonous).

And because oceans circulate just like the atmosphere does, stuff that is dumped into them just keeps spreading and spreading. Toxic chemicals are found thousands of miles from where they were dumped.

The same thing, I'm sorry to say, is true for garbage that is dumped on the land. It doesn't spread outward so much as downward. Soils get contaminated, and, as rain washes through landfills and toxic waste dumps, the polluted water filters through the soil and into the groundwater.

Although there are a few good ideas about what to do with garbage (including pumping methane out of it, to be used for fuel), the best solution is to produce less of it. So far, though, we're going the wrong direction. In 1960, each human being in the United States produced 970 pounds of garbage per year. By 1988, people in the U.S. had stepped up their garbage production to 1,450 pounds of it per person per year.

ME AND MY GARBAGE

If we're going to start heading in the *right* direction, we'll have to do two important things. One is to recycle the garbage we produce, and the other is to produce less of it to begin with.

Let's take the first one first: recycling. If you live in a community where recycling is already being done, you're lucky; all you have to do is plug into the system (and maybe your family already has). If your community does not have a program in place, find out the nearest town or city that accepts recyclables.

Many organizations collect things for recycling, and you can join one of them. Or you can encourage an organization you're already a member of to start a recycling program.

Most recycling efforts involve separating garbage into three different categories: glass (jars and bottles, rinsed out and with labels removed), newspaper, and metal (aluminum and steel or tin cans, also rinsed out and with labels removed).

Recycling not only reduces garbage but saves tremendous amounts of energy and raw materials when the same products are reused instead of being made over from scratch. Every aluminum beverage can that is recycled saves the energy equivalent of half a beverage can full of gasoline. Recycling every copy of just one Sunday edition of the *New York Times* would save seventy-five thousand trees!

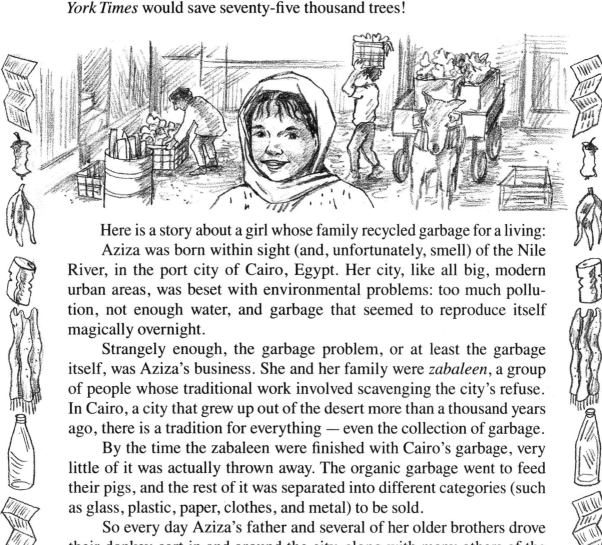

Here is a story about a girl whose family recycled garbage for a living:

Aziza was born within sight (and, unfortunately, smell) of the Nile River, in the port city of Cairo, Egypt. Her city, like all big, modern urban areas, was beset with environmental problems: too much pollution, not enough water, and garbage that seemed to reproduce itself magically overnight.

Strangely enough, the garbage problem, or at least the garbage itself, was Aziza's business. She and her family were *zabaleen*, a group of people whose traditional work involved scavenging the city's refuse. In Cairo, a city that grew up out of the desert more than a thousand years ago, there is a tradition for everything — even the collection of garbage.

By the time the zabaleen were finished with Cairo's garbage, very little of it was actually thrown away. The organic garbage went to feed their pigs, and the rest of it was separated into different categories (such as glass, plastic, paper, clothes, and metal) to be sold.

So every day Aziza's father and several of her older brothers drove their donkey cart in and around the city, along with many others of the zabaleen, picking up the discards and trash of millions of people.

Although Aziza's greatest dream was to go to school, for the present it was her and her younger brother Magdi's job to spend each day in the courtyard of their building, sorting garbage. It wasn't exactly pleasant work, so to keep herself and Magdi entertained, Aziza made up stories about some of the junk they found during the sorting. Aziza was a natural mimic and a wonderful storyteller, and sometimes she would drape herself with old rags that she found and pretend to be the people of her stories.

One day Aziza found an ancient, moth-eaten vest, which she slipped on over her own clothes to become a bent and ragged old man. She shuffled around the courtyard, wagging her head and mumbling under her breath, and slipped her fingers into the vest pocket as if to find something she had misplaced.

When her fingers actually did encounter something in the pocket, she stood up in surprise, her disguise forgotten. It was small and smooth and roundish, and she pulled it out of the pocket and held it in the palm of her hand. She and Magdi investigated it very seriously, but they couldn't figure out what it was. In any case, it clearly didn't belong in any of the sorting categories, so Aziza kept it for her own.

After she had had it for a week or so, she began to ask people what it was. Nobody knew — or seemed to care very much. But for some reason, the smooth texture and beautiful color of the object were magical to Aziza, so she held on to it. And finally, one day, she found out what it was.

Her mother had taken her, as a special treat, to visit her grandmother in another neighborhood. Just before they left to return home, Aziza showed her grandmother the treasure and asked if she knew what it was.

"That's a *leucaena* seed," her grandmother told her, "and if you put it in a can of dirt, it will make a tree."

Since Aziza had lived in a barren courtyard all her life and hadn't even seen very many trees, the thought of growing one in a can *was* magic.

Following her grandmother's instructions, Aziza got some dirt from the courtyard, where the pigs were kept, and put it in the biggest can she could find in the metal pile. She buried the seed under a layer of dirt, watered it, and then took the can up to the flat roof, where her mother and the other women in the building had their ovens.

Every day — almost every hour — she looked at the can. When the dirt got dry, she watered it. Magdi wanted to dig up the seed and see if anything was happening, but Aziza wouldn't let him. They waited and waited . . . and then they waited some more. And one day, Aziza saw a bulge under the dirt.

A few hours later, the bulge had become something green, pushing the top layer of soil aside. By the next day, Aziza could tell that it was a leaf — and the next day, she saw that it was two leaves. The miracle had happened: A tree was growing.

Although Aziza's family earned its living collecting and recycling garbage, this was the first time Aziza had seen someone's discard become something so beautiful and useful. Maybe you've had the experience of recognizing a "treasure" in somebody else's "trash" — or maybe a friend has discovered a treasure in *your* wastebasket. Either way, it's part of recycling.

The other way of taking care of the garbage problem — producing less of it — is something each of us can do. One way you can help is by *precycling* — that is, not buying things that come in complicated, useless packages that will end up right in the wastebasket. The U.S. Department of Agriculture figured out that people in the United States spent more for food packaging in one year than all the farmers in the country earned in that same year.

Here are some tips that might help you with recycling and precycling:

Trash Tips

- Collect aluminum cans. The students at one of the elementary schools in my town have been collecting beverage cans, selling them, and using the money to buy land in the Amazon rain forest, to keep it from getting deforested.

- Use recycled paper products. Many office and school supplies are now being made out of recycled paper. Be sure that the paper in your own notebooks has been recycled. You might also check with the office in your school to see if recycled paper products are being used there.

- Help ban polystyrene cups and cardboard trays at your school. Many schools have stopped using these and other products (such as plastic utensils) that are harmful to the environment. If yours hasn't, start a movement to get rid of them.

- Avoid fast-food and other carry-out restaurants that wrap foods in layers and layers of unnecessary packaging.

12

It's Up to You

As we learn more and more about our amazing Earth-ship, one thing becomes clear: We humans are just a small part of its incredible system. No matter how small a part we are, though, the human component is important. We have the power to make big mistakes. But, fortunately, we are beginning to learn that the system itself is a good teacher. It will send those mistakes right back to us, and if we pay attention, we can learn from them and change our ways.

We are busy creatures, we humans, and we always seem to find a better way to do things. Unfortunately, up to now, "better" has often meant the fastest way, the easiest way, or the way that earns the most money. We've clearly made progress of a sort, but the progress we've made has sometimes gotten us into trouble. If progress has meant "getting ahead," then maybe we could say that, from now on, it should mean "getting ahead in a way that doesn't damage the Earth-ship or any of the travelers on it."

That sounds easy enough, but it really isn't. It means that, first of all, each of us has to make changes in our own lives. It also means that at least some of us are going to have to go further than that.

Did you ever stop to think that you teach your parents things as well as vice versa? Whether you realize it or not, you're a very important source of information to them. So when you decide to make changes in your own life (as in the ways you use energy, or deal with garbage, or conserve water), let your family know what you're doing — and why.

You'd be surprised at how many important changes in our world started with just a few people. In fact, that's how a *grass-roots* effort works. It happens at the level of ordinary, everyday people like you and me, and then grows until it has the power to change things.

One person alone can accomplish a surprising amount, several people together can do even more, and a large group can move mountains. One blade of grass with one single root is a very tiny thing. But if you go out on your lawn and try to dig into the grass, you'll see what billions of grass roots can do.

A good example of that kind of power is the story of the tuna boycott in the United States. Several years ago, people in the U.S. found out that more than a hundred thousand dolphins were killed every year in the nets that were used to catch tuna. Most people hated the idea of dolphins being killed so that they could eat tuna, so they refused to buy it. In other words, they boycotted the tuna-canning companies.

The boycott was so successful that three of the leading tuna canners in the United States announced in April of 1990 that they would no longer buy or sell tuna caught by methods that also killed dolphins. So now, if you go to a store and look in the canned-fish section, you will find cans of tuna that say "dolphin safe." That is how powerful group action can be.

There are many, many ways you can put your efforts to work on behalf of the Earth-ship. You might be the kind of person who likes to do things by yourself, or you might be a person who is good at organizing things and working in public. Neither way is better than the other. Just find out what your own best contribution is, and, large or small, it will make a difference.

Now that you know about how some of Earth's systems work, one of the best planet care and repair strategies is to spend some time just being a passenger on the Earth-ship, noticing things around you. Get to know some of your fellow travelers — the ones with wings, the ones with four legs, and the ones that swim in Earth's oceans.

You can also get to know other people who are interested in taking care of the planet. You might find them in any of the many organizations that are working to care for the earth (including the one whose name is on the cover of this book). And there are many individual people, like the kids in the stories here, and others like them, who know about planet care and repair.

There have always been people who have loved and taken care of the Earth. Many of them, like John Muir (whom you read about in the first chapter), see our planet as a vast, interrelated system. In 1854, a chief of a small tribe of native people in what is now the northwestern region of the United States was asked to sell his people's land to the U.S. government. In his reply to the president of the United States, Chief Seattle explained how he and his people felt about the Earth:

"Teach your children what we have taught our children, that the Earth is our mother. Whatever befalls the Earth befalls the sons of the Earth. Man did not weave the web of life, he is merely a strand in it. Whatever he does to the web, he does to himself."

Many years later, Marjorie Kinnan Rawlings, the author of *The Yearling,* wrote, "It seems to me that the earth may be borrowed but not bought. It may be used, but not owned. It gives itself in response to love and tending, offers its seasonal flowering and fruiting. But we are tenants and not possessors. . . ."

Maybe you can get to know the Earth-ship in the same way that John Muir, Chief Seattle, and Marjorie Kinnan Rawlings did. If you pay attention to the whole system, you might find out just where your own most comfortable place in it is. And if you don't already love the Earth-ship, you just might learn to love it as you get to know it better. In the long run, you know, the best way to care for anything is to love it — and that's something you already know how to do.

Glossary

Acid rain
Precipitation that is a mixture of water vapor and chemical pollutants in the atmosphere.

Aquifer
A layer of rock, sand, or gravel where water collects under the surface of the earth.

Boycott
To refuse to deal with a company or organization in order to protest certain of its actions.

Compost
A mixture made up mostly of decayed organic matter and used as a fertilizer.

Ecosystem
All living and nonliving things that interact in a particular environment.

Energy-intensive
Requiring lots of energy.

Endangered
Threatened with extinction.

Erosion
The wearing away of soil due to the action of wind or water.

Extinct
No longer in existence.

Fossil fuel
A form of energy (such as coal, oil, or natural gas) that comes from the decayed remains of plants and animals that lived millions of years ago.

Global warming
The gradual warming of Earth's system due to atmospheric changes.

Greenhouse effect
The process in which heat energy reflected from the earth's surface is trapped inside the atmosphere.

Greenhouse gases
Substances in Earth's atmosphere that allow shortwave radiation to pass through but keep longwave radiation trapped inside.

Groundwater
Water beneath the earth's surface that supplies wells and springs.

Habitat
The natural environment in which a plant or animal lives out its life.

Hydroelectricity
Electricity produced from water power.

Land degradation
The loss of soil, or the loss of land's productivity due to human actions.

Landfill
A place where humans bury garbage or trash.

Nuclear energy
Electricity produced using energy released in a nuclear reaction.

Nuclear reaction
The process of splitting the nucleus of an atom (fission) or of combining atomic nuclei together (fusion).

Ozone layer
A layer of gas in the upper atmosphere that blocks out some of the sun's harmful radiation.

Photosynthesis
The production of chemical energy by green plants, using carbon dioxide, water, and radiant energy from the sun.

Precycling
Buying things unpackaged or in packages that reduce waste.

Radioactive
Giving off radiation, especially as the result of a nuclear reaction.

Solar radiation
Energy from the sun that is transmitted through space.

System
A group of things that interact together to form a complete whole.

Threatened
Likely to become endangered.

Index

Vicki McVey, author of the award-winning *Sierra Club Wayfinding Book* and *The Sierra Club Book of Weatherwisdom*, was raised near the Colorado Rockies and still feels at home in the mountains. She has indulged a lifelong curiosity about people and places by studying, teaching, and writing about geography. McVey holds a master's degree in cartography and a Ph.D. in cultural geography from the University of Colorado. She currently lives in the mountains near Boulder, where she writes and works as a consultant in geographic education.

Martha Weston has illustrated more than thirty books for children, including the two previous books by Vicki McVey and several titles in the Brown Paper School series published by Little, Brown. She lives in Fairfax, California, with her husband, Dick, and their children, Dory and Charley.